William Elliott's
CAROLINA SPORTS

BY

LAND AND WATER

D1607488

WILLIAM ELLIOTT

From the painting by
Thomas Sully, 1822

William Elliott's
CAROLINA SPORTS

BY

LAND AND WATER

INCLUDING

Incidents of Devil-Fishing, Wild-Cat, Deer and Bear Hunting, Etc.

WITH A NEW INTRODUCTION BY
THEODORE ROSENGARTEN

UNIVERSITY OF SOUTH CAROLINA PRESS

———————

Published in Cooperation with the Institute for Southern Studies and the South Caroliniana Society of the University of South Carolina

Published in Columbia, South Carolina, by the
University of South Carolina Press,
in cooperation with the Institute for Southern Studies and
the South Caroliniana Society

Manufactured in the United States of America

Library of Congress Cataloging-in-Publication Data

Elliott, Wm. (William), 1788–1863.
    [Carolina sports by land and water]
    William Elliott's Carolina sports by land and water :
including incidents of devil-fishing, wild-cat, deer, and
bear hunting, etc. / with a new introduction by Theodore
Rosengarten.
        p.   cm. — (Southern classics series)
    Originally published: 1846.
    ISBN 0–87249–987–1 (pbk. : acid-free)
    1. Fishing—South Carolina. 2. Hunting—South
Carolina. 3. Outdoor life—South Carolina—History—
19th century. I. Title. II. Title: Carolina sports by
land and water. III. Series.
SK125.E5   1994
799′.09757—dc20   93–31299
                                                              CIP

CONTENTS

William Elliott's Carolina Sports by Land and Water

GENERAL EDITOR'S PREFACE

WILLIAM ELLIOTT'S essays on hunting and fishing present readers with two fascinating perspectives on life in the antebellum South. On one level, his tales are robust accounts of outdoor life in the wild places of the South Carolina lowcountry. But, as Theodore Rosengarten's splendid introduction to this edition shows, the essays also tell us much—more, perhaps, than Elliott intended—about social relations in the era, and especially about the always tentative, sometimes precarious, interaction between slaveholders and slaves. A classic account of sporting life, the book also underscores the growing disquietude among members of a society undergoing profound changes.

John G. Sproat
General Editor, *Southern Classics*

INTRODUCTION

ONE fine October day, in 1837, while waiting for
his hounds to rouse a deer, William Elliott killed
two bears with one shot. Unexpected, four bears in
all had run out from the cover of a swamp onto a
piece of high ground where Elliott was standing,
bridle in hand, straining to hear the dogs. Startled,
but instinctually prepared, Elliott leapt onto his
horse to try to cut the bears off from regaining the
swamp. He hadn't gone far when two of the bears
turned and headed toward him, not to attack, but
to escape the hounds whose baying could be heard
in the distance. After advancing to within twenty
yards of the hunter, the larger of the bears stopped
and looked at him "full in the face." The smaller
bear, "as if prompted by curiosity, reared himself
on his hind legs and looked inquisitively over the
shoulder of the leader," much like a man would. As
the heads of the two bears came in line, Elliott raised
his shotgun, aimed between the eyes of the larger
bear, and fired. Instantly the foremost bear disappeared, while the yearling bear uttered a "cry of
distress" and rolled out of sight. At the spot where
the first bear had stood, Elliott found the animal
still in an upright posture, motionless with its head
sunk on its knees. "He was stone dead!" exclaimed
the man who shot him. It wasn't long before Elliott's
hunting buddies were crowding around and offering

their congratulations. They wouldn't believe him, however, about wounding a second bear with the same shot, but soon enough the hounds led the hunters to a thicket where the young bear lay dead.

By Elliott's time bears seldom were seen in the South Carolina lowcountry, and few were the men who could say they had ever laid eyes on one, much less shot two with one barrel. But Elliott's pleasure was spoiled when a companion called him lucky. "What a damper!" sighed Elliott, "to tell a man who was priding himself on having made a magnificent shot, that it was nothing but luck." "Be it so," he snapped at his jealous friend, "but when you have beaten this shot and killed three bears with one barrel, let me know it, I pray you, and I will try my luck again." Poking fun at himself for going around in a state of "wounded self-love," Elliott would have the last laugh, for the spot where he shot the bears would henceforth be known as "The Bear Stand."

All this happened in the vicinity of Chee-ha, a low, wet, fertile neck of land between the Ashepoo and Combahee Rivers, about forty miles southwest of Charleston. Elliott was an absentee landlord, and he used the occasion of visiting his outlying plantations to go hunting. It was clearly the hunt, and not the inspection of his property, that his heart was set on. In fact, on four separate visits to Chee-ha he spent a total of two hours on his nearby plantation. The rest of the time was consumed chasing deer at a furious pace.

What made him such an avid hunter? Heredity, was his answer; he inherited "the tastes of my grandfather, as well as his lands." On one parcel of that inheritance, his father, William Elliott, had raised the first big crop of Sea Island cotton in South Carolina and grown famously wealthy in the 1790s. Elliott followed in his paternal footsteps, both by creating new wealth and cultivating the honorable old pastimes. Hunting and fishing were his birthrights. Of course, the poor hunted and fished too, but for different reasons and with different customs and resources. Why the southern man hunted was a subject that fascinated historian Wilbur J. Cash. Unable to put his finger on a motive, Cash generalized in *The Mind of the South* (1941) that the southerner, by which he meant the white man, hunted "for the same reason that, in his youth and often into late manhood, he ran spontaneous and unpremeditated foot-races, wrestled, drank Gargantuan quantities of raw whisky, let off wild yells, and hunted the possum:—because the thing was already in his mores when he emerged from the backwoods, because on the frontier it was the obvious thing to do, because he was a hot, stout fellow, full of blood and reared to outdoor activity, because of a primitive zest for the pursuit at hand."

The aristocratic Elliott hardly fits Cash's description. He disdained the lowly possum, and, while he was a big talker, he did not like to call attention to himself by raising his voice; he drank his share of fine wines and brandies, but he did not guzzle or

touch corn liquor to his lips; the backwoods had
never been his habitat—his people had crossed the
Atlantic and kept close to the seashore when they
got here. Still, he was intimate with a wilderness—
the woods and swamps between the plantations—
which he coveted and mastered by killing large
animals. And when it came to running races, Elliott
had outstanding speed. He was the fastest runner in
his class at Harvard. What appealed to him most
about outdoor sports was the premium they put on
athleticism. Take, for example, devil-fishing, the subject of his best-known essay. The sport consists of
harpooning a three- to five-ton creature in the ray
family from a small boat which the wounded beast
pulls at breakneck speed across the water until it
dies of exhaustion. You have to be quick and strong
to plant the harpoon in the back of the quarry, and
it takes mental and physical toughness to toss and
tumble across a billowy bay. Nobody ate devil-fish—
just as the white hunters did not eat bear; neither
was the devil-fish hunted for trophy. The object of
the sea-hunt was the thrill of the chase and of the
ride on the back of a beast of seemingly supernatural
strength. Elliott liked to contrast the intense emotions generated by devil-fishing with the polite sen-
sations that come with trout fishing and fox-hunting
in the tamer North and in England. The sport was
too new to be traditional—Elliott claims to have
been the first to kill a devil-fish in Port Royal Sound
in 1817. And like Elliott's killing of the bears, the
slaying of devil-fish had no ceremony about it. The

hunter did not ask their permission to kill them or feel impoverished by their deaths. Elliott's world was pre-Civil War, pre-Darwin, guileless and brazen, in contrast to the defeated, haunted, postwar world of William Faulkner's great hunting tale, *The Bear* (1942).

Yet, change had begun, and Elliott was sensitive to the signs. The golden age of Sea Island cotton, of fantastic profits and lavish spending, had been cut short by economic recession, though by acting shrewdly men of Elliott's class still could count on adding to their estates or, at worst, living off the fat of their gut. The populations of plants and animals once regarded as plentiful had begun to fall off through overhunting and single-crop farming that starved out every other living thing. Imperceptible to people who valued economic growth above all, the drift toward scarcity filled Elliott with the dread of loss at least fifteen years before the War. Coincidentally, as his athleticism waned, he spent less time hunting and fishing and more time pursuing the elixir of health at spas and invalid colonies.

Well before his sixtieth birthday he had begun worrying what people would think of him when he was gone. The most significant thing he could imagine leaving for posterity was his book of sporting stories. By 1845, when he found a publisher who would take them, he was articulating a second motive. He wanted to show slavery in its true light, a good light, he thought. The year he had harpooned his first devil-fish, organized abolitionism barely existed. In fact, four out of five members of abolition societies were living in the South and they had no voice in national politics or culture. In the 1840s the movement caught on in the North, and on his frequent visits to New York and New England, Elliott felt personally criticized and welcome only for the money he had come to spend. Harvard, where men of pro-slavery convictions used to gather openly, no longer gave him refuge. He felt condemned for the circumstances of his birth, not for anything he had done. And he knew in his bones where this would all end.

He shows us slavery in two settings: First, in the wild, where the black man plays the part of servant and helper, rower of the boat and driver of the hounds, a pliable, likeable fellow who is witty and practical and able to think for himself if need be. Second, we meet the slaves at his Chee-ha plantation, full-time residents who appear to belong to the land rather than to their owner, who is but an infrequent visitor. Master and slaves are strangers to each other, and Elliott's impressions of them are not flattering. His hunts at Chee-ha are great successes, judging by the catch, the thrills, and the stories that come out of them. But the visit to the plantation is a disaster, a descent into a dark underworld peopled by rude, devious, inhospitable creatures who get under Elliott's skin like chiggers.

Not surprisingly, Elliott tries to leave there as soon as possible, and in his anxiety to escape he trips over his tongue, so to speak, demeaning himself in an exchange of nonsensical remarks which he would recollect and utilize later in the safety of his study for comic purposes. Yet something serious had happened; in fact, the encounter is a key to the book, its chief source of suspense and complexity. The purpose of the master's visit, broadly speaking, is simply for him to show his face. He has come to see for himself what is going on and what his overseer has been lying to him about for six months. But he really doesn't want to know. He is torn between affirming his inheritance by demonstrating his authority, and wanting to run away from the place and avoid the obligations his inheritance confers on him. The placement of the bear story right after the fateful meeting on the plantation gives it the singular burden of redeeming the master in his own eyes, and shoring up his claim to the land which can be no more than a share, even if it is the lion's share, because the slaves have a claim to it too, by virtue of actual possession. At one level *Carolina Sports* can be read with naturalistic delight as a group of adventure stories set in an exotic American milieu which is vividly and imaginatively rendered. At another level, the stories are rescued from the province of the tall tale by the creeping thought that owning slaves is a curse, to slave and master alike.

Whether Elliott can salvage his stature, or whether he is doomed to feel the hollowness of his rule, is the conclusive drama of the book. No matter what the outcome, the conflict subverts the defense of slavery Elliott says he intends to make. Perhaps

Elliott succeeded in convincing the converted. But
no writer writes for us what he wrote for his contemporaries, and Elliott's intentions can be fruitfully
scrutinized by readers armed with knowledge and
questions generated in our own day. There is no
doubt about the seriousness of the problem that
blows up in Elliott's face at his Chee-ha plantation.
Nor is there any doubt about the parody that suf-
fuses and leavens the stories, a spate of self-criticism
directed against an overweaning vanity that let in
more light than it shut out.

As attached as he was to slavery, Elliott loved the
Union too. He grew up in the years of intense na-
tionalism between the two wars with England, and
for him the first revolution was the only revolution.
All his adult life he denounced "nearsighted oppor-
tunists" who fought federal authority or plotted to
secede from the nation. When he went off to Harvard
in 1806, the trans-Atlantic slave trade had two years
to run, and the question of ending internal slavery,
which had perturbed the writers of the Constitution,
had receded behind visions of cotton as high as
Arctic snow drifts. Elliott was a southern boy—his
parents sent him boxes of oranges and barrels of rice
grown on the family's plantations—but his southern-
ness did not set him apart. He felt he belonged, and
when he left Harvard before graduating in 1808, he
expected to return. But his father died suddenly,
and young William stayed home to take over the
elder Elliott's responsibilities.

In 1816 Elliott fell in love with fourteen-year-old Ann Hutchinson Smith, daughter of Thomas Rhett Smith and Ann Rebecca Skirving. The betrothed spent a year apart, filling the time writing letters to each other—a habit they would cultivate to his dying day—and married when she turned fifteen. Her parents gave the newlyweds a one-thousand-acre plantation with thirty-five slaves, and through his wife Elliott would acquire in all five plantations to go with the four he inherited. For half a century he planted rice and cotton on his ever-growing estate, trebling his wealth and siring nine children among whom later to divide his riches. Planter by profession and writer by avocation, Elliott was also a legislator, by dint of family tradition. From 1814 to 1832 he held his father's old seat in the state house of representatives and then served in the state senate. He deemed himself "an honorable representative of the planting interest," and his program consisted of defending the planters' disproportionate power in the legislature. But that wasn't enough to satisfy his constituents who came under the sway of hotheads and wanted him to vote to nullify federal tariff law in South Carolina. Elliott refused, and quit the senate. He opposed nullification, he said, because it was unconstitutional. He believed the controversy was making the state a laughingstock, scaring away investment and immigrants and threatening property values. Conscious of his own narcissism, he readily spied its symptoms in others, and observed that "the excitement which agitates the country [is] absolutely got up for the personal aggrandizement of certain characters."

He came home to Beaufort in 1832 and finding the political climate not to his liking, he moved his family to Oak Lawn Plantation, the opulent northerly outpost of his estate, on the Edisto River. But there was no avoiding conflict. Elliott fell into a bitter quarrel with the Rhett family over drainage rights to Middle Place, on the Ashepoo River. He coined the phrase "greedy as Rhetts" to characterize his Beaufort neighbors who fed their cattle on his cotton. There's no telling what the Rhetts said about him, but personal feelings spilled into politics, and like a tarbaby, the dispute drew to itself anyone who came near, friends and lawyers, cotton factors and in-laws.

Another arena of conflict for Elliott was the education of his children. For his sons, the problem was that there were no suitable schools of higher education in the lowcountry and, as it turned out, the boys were unprepared to leave home. Upon William, his first-born, Elliott placed the hope of becoming "the literary man in the family." It was William, or no one, Elliott wrote to him. "Your brother Tom can be nothing but a planter, for he would never study." As for brother Ralph, he did not show an aptitude to "sustain the reputation of the name." With the hopes for William came the warning that "Nothing is more certain, than that my children will have to rely on their own character and exertions for their support in life."

Wealthy, and still adding to his fortune, Elliott grew increasingly pessimistic about the future of agriculture. Even as prices were rising he held to the lesson of the recession that had smothered profits like a thick blanket in 1818: Things cannot be as good as they appear to be, and furthermore they are not. Apparently, Elliott thought he was throwing his money away by paying William's bills at Harvard and officially withdrew him from school, blaming the kind of "disordered health" that comes from drinking and carousing. When William complained that he had been "sent too young," Elliott despaired, "What was I to do with you?" He could not send him to Columbia "for the idleness and vice that I knew to prevail there," so he packed him off to familiar Cambridge, "the only remaining resource." Ralph appears to have resisted education too, judging by his father's complaint about how hard it was to make "any youth in this southern country feel that he needs any instruction, or requires the least restraint." Ralph was enrolled at the University of Virginia, under a sensible regime where the young men handed over their spending money to a patron.

For the girls, the problem was the stultifying atmosphere of the plantation, the dearth of social and cultural opportunities. They were not expected to go off to a university or to leave the premises of home even for primary instruction. Once they learned to read and write, to sew and play piano, the plantation, in their father's eyes, was no place for girls of their talents. Travel was the remedy—to the spas and to the great cities of the North. Life in the lowcountry was not enough for them, as it was not for their father.

Travel was expensive, time-consuming, and exhausting. By ship or coach, the traveler could expect to receive a good jostling and bad food. Elliott was routinely "swindled by hackmen," and having arrived at his destination—illustrious Saratoga, for example—he and his daughters had to "wend our way among sharks and pickpockets." Elliott's contemporary and friend William Grayson, also an arch defender of slavery and foe of secession, described in his autobiography, *Witness to Sorrow*, written early in the Civil War but not published until 1990, how his family spent a month among "the summer idlers" at Saratoga. They "inhaled the dust of the streets; drank the Congress water, rushed with the crowd to dinner and supper; occupied a room ten foot square; slept on a hard mattress of straw and corn shucks, and paid for all these enjoyments the long bill that Northern watering places inflict on Southern simpletons." On top of all these indignities, Grayson, Elliott, and the legion of southern travelers who "fluttered like moths" around the northern springs, felt humiliated by the discrepancy in wealth between the North and South. "Everything impresses the idea of great wealth and forces a southerner to feel his poverty," Elliott wrote home in the summer of 1836. The discrepancy did not abate, and over the years Elliott repeatedly compared northern energy and manufacturing with southern lethargy and underdevelopment. "We of the South sleep upon our advantages," he wrote to his wife, after visiting the factory town of Lowell, Massachusetts. He marveled that a place he remembered from his youth as "nothing but a naked sandy plain" had sprouted a town of 18,000. "Whole squares have been beautifully built up of brick and granite," he observed at stop after stop across New England. "A month's tour through these states would wake us all," he continued, justifying the time he was spending away by what he was learning.

Paradoxically, the more that political changes made him feel like a southerner, the more he looked to the North for a model of economic development, and the more that anti-slavery enthralled the North, the less willing he was to criticize his homeland openly and directly. Not that he ever gave a thought to abandoning agriculture and slavery. He wanted to emulate the North by introducing labor-saving machines, such as water-driven saws and pumps, on his plantations. He made it his business to learn from the North how to make his enterprises more profitable. At the same time he helped the North by spending the profits from rice and cotton on carpets, clothing, wine, and furniture.

To the pull of the North was added the push from the South, in the form of the threat of disease, so that Elliott continued to flee the southern summers right up to the Civil War. He wrote home from New York in October, 1858, that the city "is crowded with homesick Southerners anxious to go home—but un-

willing to take the risk." Elliott was by nature a
hypochondriac. He may have worried for his daughters' intellectual development, but his chief motive
in leaving home and hopping from spa to spa was
to restore his health. He suffered chronically from
an unidentified throat affliction and what he called
rheumatic headache. He sought a water cure for
conditions as diverse as bronchitis, gout, shattered
nerves, and vertigo. On a trip to Saratoga in 1845
he carried a copy of R. T. Claridge's *Hydrophy: or
the Cold Water Cure, as practiced by Vincent Preis-
snits, at Garefenberg, Silesia, and Austria*, which
advised sufferers to take cold baths to separate dis-
eased from healthy matter in the body.

Elliott preferred the hot treatments, and they
seemed to do him good. Though the regimens at
Warm Springs and White Sulphur Springs, in western Virginia, worked for him, he preferred the company at Saratoga, where the chief activity of every
day was changing one's clothes for the endless meals,
balls, and wine parties. When he felt well he would
show off his dancing skills and receive the compli-
ments of ladies who did not believe his age. He was
one of "the lions," and while he joked about rubbing
shoulders with "the most distingués," he counted
himself among "the highest aristocracy." He felt
polluted by social contact with the commonality.
Once, as he wrote to his wife from Charleston (where
he had gone, among other reasons, to find a publisher
for *Carolina Sports*), he was invited to a ball where
"vulgar people in abundance will doubtless attend

. . . and as pitch defileth." He liked Paris, where he spent the summer of 1855, because people knew their place, lower-class individuals did not approach unless asked, and when they did they knew their manners. Seven years had passed since the working people of Paris had tried to put egalité into practice and lost their heads for their trouble. The lone sour note on his European trip occurred on a jaunt to Switzerland; at the castle of Chillon, he saw where "that reptile woman Mrs. [Harriet Beecher] Stowe, (who has filled Europe with her defamations of her native country) had carved her name along side of Byron's," an act that appalled Elliott and left him sputtering.

With Elliott away some years for the greater part of the growing season, someone had to manage in his place. His wife governed the house while his slaves and lands were put under the care of hired overseers. But such a situation was just a beginning to his problems. "He knows little of the world who knows not that overseers are to be overseen," experience had taught him. Even when Elliott was home he was an absentee of sorts to all but one of his plantations. Getting from one plantation to another, dozens of miles away, over miserable roads, was a trial Elliott learned to pass up. From near or far, the absentee had all the problems of the resident planter, with several more besides. Drought, flood, insects, food supply, slave morale, market forces outside his control, and problems of human relations. It seemed Elliott was never free of the difficulty of

finding competent people to look out for his interests.
A lifetime of looking had left him with a "low esti-
mate of human honesty." Good men must not have
gone into the overseer's trade. The ones Elliott hired
made a specialty of seeking "only the business of
absentees." They knew how to get what they wanted
without striving to make a decent crop, by robbing
the planter of anything of value he foolishly left
around. "The moment my back has been turned in
the summer," wrote Elliott, "I have been fleeced." In
Saratoga, Flat Rock, or Paris, Elliott desponded of
getting accurate information about the state of his
crops. The news that reached him before the harvest
was invariably bad. "I fear I must come home to lost
crops and to severe economy," he wrote with ritu-
alistic pessimism from Philadelphia in October,
1839. Whosoever was supplying him with news was
trying to keep expectations low, and Elliott went
along with the game. Results in the end usually did
not turn out "so ruinous as I had feared," and the
planter made a profit. He never ceased making profits and he never ceased complaining. Sometimes he
rehired a man he knew was cheating him. "I have to
swallow my wounded pride," he wrote from a distance, "and reengage Sanders. The Negroes if un-
controlled would burn down all the houses." There
was no indication of affections-that-bind between
Elliott and his people. Far in the past was the age
when master and slaves saw each other every day,
or worked together at the frontier tasks it took to
establish a plantation. They were strangers to each

other now. The blacks still obeyed the white man when he came around, but only because they had to, and their obedience was tainted with cheek and indifference.

"Of all races," Elliott wrote, articulating the nineteenth-century position, "the negro is the least able to go unwatched." Why employ African Americans at all, then, if getting them to do their work was so problematic? Elliott's reason, in a word, was climate. "If the white man could labor in the region of malaria, the labor of blacks would not be resorted to," he argued boldly. The climate was fixed; southerners had no alternative. Northerners did not understand; abolition would turn the rice and cotton lands to desert. Even slave owners did not know how fortunate they were to have access to African slaves. On his trip to France in 1855, Elliott studied the prospects of competition for Sea Island cotton from Algeria. "The climate & soil suit," he wrote home. "All that saves us is their want of *negroes!*" White men would not work in the heat, and Africans, in his felicitous phrase, were "not comeatable." If the American people would only stop to think they could save themselves from disaster. Taking to the streets of New York in search of a publisher for his book of sports, he announced, "I desire to place the institution of slavery in the South on its true basis, that exigency of climate—"

Not that he expected to change many minds, or was under the illusion that he had written a bestseller. But he understood that the market shared the mood of the day, and that every book by a southern author was interrogated for its position on slavery. And he understood something else: that while the pages of *Carolina Sports* devoted to portraying slavery could be counted on two hands, and that in another era readers would hurry over them to get on with the tales of the chase, slavery was indeed the bedrock of his life, the creator of his wealth and the liberator of his time, the system that gave him the power, and the culture that gave him the prerogative of reserving forests and swamps that other people might put to other uses, as hunting grounds for himself and his friends.

"Devil Fishing" first appeared in 1829 in the Baltimore periodical *American Turf Register and Sporting Magazine*. "Drum Fishing" followed in 1830. All the stories contained in the 1846 edition of *Carolina Sports* had appeared in other places, published under the pen names Piscador—an alias used by Isaak Walton, whose classic *The Compleat Angler* was a favorite of Elliott—and Venator. The publisher of the 1859 edition commissioned six illustrations and had Elliott add "The Sea-Serpent" in an effort to broaden the book's appeal by recounting incidents that reportedly took place in New England waters. It is this edition that the current volume follows. The sea-serpent story, but not the illustrations, appeared in the 1918 edition published by the State Company, in Columbia, South Carolina. Editions published in 1967 and 1977 have kept the book in print, though its existence continues to be a well-kept secret.

Marc Bloch, the great French historian, once observed that "the migration of manuscripts is, in itself, an extremely interesting object of study" because it corresponds exactly to the "vicissitudes of life." The same might be said for the travels of a book. In fact, the publishing history of *Carolina Sports* tells a great deal about the prevailing myths and needs of different generations. Elliott's friends did not rally around the book as he had hoped. William Gilmore Simms, a defender of the old traditions, was put off by its "excessive vivacity" and its deficiency "in the art which conceals art." *Carolina Sports* was too noisy for him. It "wants," wrote Simms in the *Southern Quarterly Review*, "the grace of ease" which is the mark of a genuine aristocrat. True, the prose zips along on kinetic verbs such as "rush" and "devour," "leap" and "plunge," and there are passages that make one picture the author in the act of writing, but the zany product, with its archaic expressions and pompous classical allusions, reads like a conscious attempt to sound old, English, well-read.

The sporting sketches invite comparison with the raucous frontier tales of Elliott's and Simms's contemporaries J. J. Hooper and T. B. Thorpe, southern humorists who were busy creating an American literature crafted in local vernacular and peopled with brash, colorful characters. Hooper's most important work, *Some Adventures of Captain Simon Suggs*, may be the first American picaresque novel. It appeared as a whole in 1845 after the pieces had debuted, like Elliott's, in sporting magazines. (Hooper later published a hunting book, *Dog and Gun: A Few Loose Chapters on Shooting*.) Thorpe's great short story, "The Big Bear of Arkansas," was much admired by Faulkner and by enough readers in Thorpe's own day to win him a small fame which lasted longer in the North where he was born and to where he returned in 1852 after losing the election for superintendent of education in Louisiana.

The wilderness Elliott knew was not on the frontier. The frontier, Indian country, the backwoods were far away from Elliott's world, a world of educated white men who had been sent off to school and who, when they returned, stayed in the habit of reading. Elliott could not stop himself from showing off his learning. But if he had evolved into an apparent Englishman, it was not the Englishman of England but the Englishman of some imperial outpost, like the governor of one of the Antilles, perhaps, who clings to the language, metaphors, and circumlocutions of the mother tongue while back at home everything is changing.

To an 1850 reprint of *Carolina Sports*, Elliott affixed a five-line preface aligning himself with the antiquarians by affirming his "adherence to the old signatures," Piscator and Venator, so as to "avoid the imputation of egotism, which necessarily attaches itself to the narration of one's own adventures under his proper name." The sea-serpent story, added to the New York edition of 1859, reads more like a tall tale than a true adventure; furthermore, the mock heroism and frivolity which precede the unmasking of the monster undermines the artistic humbling of the hunters in the second part of the book. Probably the Yankee publishers hoped the comedy would boost sales. Perhaps, at a time when anti-southern feeling was running high, they were covertly editorializing by projecting an image of superstitious aristocrats who spent their time chasing chimeras and practiced planting on the side.

In the introduction to the London edition of 1867, James Spence, a diehard Confederate supporter, found nothing funny in the portrait of a lost world. This edition appeared in the hated days of Reconstruction when, according to Spence, "even as Rachel, the South sits mourning for her children and will not be comforted." Elliott's fishing and hunting stories apparently conveyed to the friends of the mourners, in Spence's words, "the principles of truth and justice" now prostrate under the federal occupation but which would one day win out and command the world's admiration.

Paradise lost became paradise regained in the 1918 republication by the State Company, edited by Elliott's grandson Ambrose Elliott Gonzales, who happened to be the publisher of the *State* newspaper. Gonzales reprinted Spence's memorial and fortified it with his own attack on Reconstruction. "Backed by federal bayonets," he reported, referring not to Americans in the trenches of France but to that war

of greater immediacy fought more than a half century earlier, "the slaves of a brave and high-spirited
people . . . were put in power over their kindly
masters." In this interpretation of history the slaves
are nonentities, creatures without qualities; sympathy and interest rest exclusively with the slaveholders. Gonzales was emboldened by the popular culture. American opinion makers had come around:
The South's way had been the right way after all.
The civilization of the Old South, with its rules of
conduct and traditional hierarchy, was the best kind
of world for everyone. Taking a swipe at immigrants,
and forgetting the black half the population, Gonzales styled "the south, with its homogeneous English
speaking people" as "the balance wheel, the very
heart of the nation."

Fifty years later, *Carolina Sports* was rescued
from this doctrine and returned to the world of
sport when the ARNO Press, in New York, published the book as part of "The Abercrombie & Fitch
Library of rediscovered works by great sportsmen
of the past." Thus *Carolina Sports* joined a list with
The Compleat Angler, Paul Hyde Bonner's *The
Glorious Morning* and *Aged in the Woods*, and half-
forgotten classic accounts of big-game hunts, polar
explorations, and ocean racing. The ARNO Press
version is a facsimile of the Charleston original of
1846. A 1977 republication by the Attic Press, in
Greenwood, South Carolina, follows the New York
edition of 1859. Neither of these modern editions
contains anybody's words but Elliott's, no one else's

packaging. What you get is Elliott—a self-conscious aristocrat writing feverish prose about chasing and killing game on the malarial coast of South Carolina before the overthrow of slavery.

He wrote about other subjects, too, particularly politics and agriculture, and his New York publisher tinkered with the idea of fattening the sporting book by including some of the agricultural essays. Elliott strenuously objected, and the publisher backed off. The subjects were too different, Elliott felt, and so was the writer's voice. The hunter-fisherman has to win his spurs each time he goes out, and his stories are heavy with expectation. He goes through trial and error and the catch is his reward because it has tested him. The agricultural speaker is didactic and dry. Known for his wealth and for the prices his cotton and rice fetch at the market, he is a logical man to turn to if you are looking for advice. People read him because they want to be rich like him and think he might let them in on his secrets. Elliott wrote in praise of crop diversity, attacking cotton and rice monocultures and calling for increases of wheat and small grains, indigo, pasture-fed beef. In his 1856 address to the State Agricultural Society he lectured on the virtues of good drainage, heavy manuring, and fine tillage. One-quarter of the forty-four page oration was a rigorous defense of slavery, since slaves were as necessary as the soil.

The reforms he advocated were dreams when set against the wasteful and inefficient realities he discovered on his own plantations. The agricultural

ideal runs head-up against natural calamities and
human resistance, while the hunting ideal grows to
a passion in the grind, sickness, boredom, and lone-
liness of the long plantation days. *Carolina Sports*
is a book about high times, special moments worth
living and re-living. In his letters, beautifully edited
and thoughtfully annotated by Beverly Scafidel but
as yet unpublished, Elliott confides his deep feelings
for the book and his proud hopes, held back by false
modesty like a leaky balloon trying to hold helium.
The four hundred twenty-four letters represent, of
course, only those that have survived, and we should
assume that some number did not, and that some
that did have not come to light. The point is, Elliott
was a prolific letter writer, and the letters are an
essential record of his thought. I have quoted liber-
ally from them in this essay and can only say that
it is a shame they are not generally available. But
transcriptions of the originals can be read in their
entirety at both the Thomas Cooper Library and the
South Caroliniana Library at the University of
South Carolina, Columbia. The first letter is to Elliott's father, from Cambridge, dated February 6,
1808, thanking him for "the oranges and potatoes
you were so good to send me," describing the senior
year curriculum at Harvard, and noting apologeti-
cally that "There is neither a dancing nor a fencing
master" in the area; the last letter is to his wife,
dated New Year's Day, 1863, and sent from Charleston, where he would die four weeks and five days
later, expressing with a cheer already sobered by

the longevity of the war the assurance that "If we [Confederates] succeed in our battles now in progress in the West, our horizon will be greatly brighter than before." The last words of a man who loved life, in spite of its griefs and disappointments.

The settings for the fishing and hunting stories are wild places still. Far fewer people live in the Chee-ha region today than lived there in Elliott's day, since the plantations have ceased producing staple crops and the descendants of the slaves have moved away. The deer are more abundant today than they were in the 1840s, when Elliott noticed a decline. The area he hunted has been set aside by agreement between recent owners and the Nature Conservancy in a vast preserve of old and new wilderness called the ACE Basin. ACE is an acronym denoting the three rivers which flood and drain the seaward edge of the coastal plain, the very rivers which once bordered Elliott's domain: the Ashepoo, Combahee, and Edisto. The rivers he fished were southwest of these, and emptied into Port Royal Sound. Many lowcountry streams might better be called "arms of the sea" because they carry salt water inland and out again without meeting significant sources of fresh water. They have never communicated with a productive backcountry or become roads of trade, and we owe their naturalness today to their commercial insignificance.

The fishing stories make up the first half of *Carolina Sports,* and more than two-thirds of these pages

are devoted to the thrills of devil-fishing. Yet if
planters had to name their favorite denizen of the
deep it would be the drum fish, "the largest scale
fish in America," whose drumming noise during the
spawning season was reveille to their ears. In mid-
April, at cotton-planting time, they would drop
everything, slip their freshly caulked and painted
boats into the water, and head to their pet spots in
Broad River. Drum fish were running. Delicious to
eat, drum were pursued mainly because they gave
great sport, attacking the hooks and fighting fran-
tically until pulled onto the boat. Elliott enjoyed
the social atmosphere and the zealous competition
for the biggest catch. "Imagine yourself afloat on
our beautiful bay," Elliott reminisced, "the ocean
before you—the islands encircling you—and a great
fleet of forty or fifty fishing boats (their awnings
glistening in the sun) riding sociably around." Tranquil enough, until the first drum strikes a line. Boats
nearest the lucky one quickly run up alongside,
indicating to everyone the location of the school.

Drum fish in spring, sheepshead in summer, bass
in autumn gave three seasons of sport. (Sheepshead
are deep-bodied, spiny-finned relatives of porgies,
equipped with broad incisor teeth for crushing mol-
lusks.) In chatty, anecdotal sketches rich in natural
history and local wisdom, Elliott recounts the pleasures and perils of fishing for sheepshead and bass.
They set the table, so to speak, for the hunting stories
that follow, by completing the author's brief for sea-

fishing and arousing the reader's desire for a more continuous narrative.

A tale about hunting wild-cat in a hinterland only three miles from the old town of Beaufort opens the second half of the book. The hunters' guns are charged with every kind of shot in preparation "for whatever game might present itself." The sportsmen are also armed with knives, horses, dogs, servants; the cats have their wiles. There follow the four sketches of day hunts taken at Chee-ha—on separate occasions, but the accounts are linked by titles, themes, moods, and effects into the narrative of a single extended excursion. On the first day's hunt, Elliott bags a deer by kicking it in the head from his horse, then dismounting and killing it with his knife. "Another Day at Chee-ha," the second piece, is a hymn to wilderness and a slap at the northern sport of shooting coop-raised birds who have been released into protective covers.

Then comes the story of Elliott's fateful visit to his Chee-ha plantation. First he comes upon the overseer, a white man, and finds him feverish and dull-witted, reduced to pudding by the heat, insects, whiskey, and months of fraternizing with the slaves. *They* have somehow stayed fat and healthy. They've been getting a full ration of food, but Elliott cannot tell from a glance what work they've done to deserve it.

"I enter the barn-yard," he begins, cautiously, as if he were on someone else's property. "The driver doffs his hat and draws a long scrape of the right

foot by way of welcome; and the glossy-backed operatives hedge me about with a circle of flail sticks
by way of salute." He feels trapped already. The
hands are taking a break from their task of threshing
the cut rice; they are looking him over. He returns
the favor. "What greasy-looking rogues," he observes
through pitiless eyes. He is repelled by "their grosser
bodies" which have been "nourished," as only creatures of their race could be, "by the dank vapors of
the swamp." What kind of encounter is this? Where
does Elliott find the words to describe what he sees,
what he feels? Is this all the human sympathy this
man of science, lover of books, this alumnus of Harvard, can muster?

Elliott tries to extract information about the crop.
Is it really as good as it looks? The slaves, in turn,
want things from him—cloth, shoes, the kinds of
goods that flow like water at Warm Springs and
Saratoga. The master has no patience for their petitions; he wants to get away as fast as he can. His
conversation turns slapstick, but he himself is not
amused. These people, with their chronic demands,
are a pain in the neck. They assault his senses, prick
his conscience, and in general make him feel bad.
Beneath him socially, not even on the same ladder,
they exercise a strange power over him. They force
him to abandon his good opinion of himself and
somehow they make him feel mortal. On the hunt he
is God-like, the taker and occasionally preserver of
life, omnipotent in his knowledge of animals and
their habitats, but here in the slave quarters on a

civilized piece of ground, he is alien and extraneous, valued only for his gold. Everybody wants a piece of him and he, who owes a large piece of himself to each one of them, wants out.

He never does regain his composure that day, and nearly makes a fool of himself in front of his hunting companions by threatening to jump in the river and recover a dead deer floating downstream on the current. From here to the end of the book, despite Elliott's steadfast attention "to the track of our narrative," despite the wonderful bear story and a discerning conclusion about the future of the planter class in the ecology of Beaufort, it is hard to shake loose from the scene in the barnyard at Chee-ha. Things just could not go on this way. We know it. And if we read between the ink spots we know that Elliott knew it. I am reminded of something George Orwell wrote about watching a file of Senegalese soldiers, "the blackest Negroes in Africa," pass by his hotel in Morocco in 1940. "There is one thought which every white man (and in this connection it doesn't matter a twopence if he calls himself a socialist) thinks when he sees a black army marching past. 'How much longer can we go on kidding these people? How long before they turn their guns in the other direction.' It was curious, really. Every white man there had this thought stowed somewhere or other in his mind. . . . It was a kind of secret which we all knew and were too clever to tell; only the Negroes didn't know it."

I don't say that Elliott intended to betray his

unease over slavery. I don't believe he tried to ex-
press it, but he did so anyway. And he wasn't concerned with right and wrong, but with physical
danger. Did he wonder as he stood in the barnyard
encircled by his field hands, how long before they
turn their flail sticks on me? I bet he did, from the
fact of how quickly he departed, and the sweat he
was thrown into. As with all good writing, the mean-
ing is what the writer arrives at, not what he begins
with. Writing was a process that took Elliott to a
better place of understanding than where he would
have been stuck had he succeeded in writing what
he thought he knew at the beginning. His readers
might not have appreciated his dilemma in 1846, or
1859, or 1918. But by thinking about it now, we may
come away savoring the book's complexity and en-
dearing disunity.

The ironies of the story surrounding the publication of the 1859 edition would have delighted Anton
Chekhov. Elliott never stopped trying to find a
publisher in New York who, and only who, could
"give the book currency." He was laboring, he told
his wife, in a climate of "contemptuous indifference
to any Southern book." Lippincott in Philadelphia
turned him down and he almost lost heart. But then,
as now, it was a matter of whom one knew. Enter
Elliott's friend, J. E. DeBow, editor of the important
southern commercial magazine *DeBow's Review*.
DeBow introduced Elliott to the firm of Derby &
Jackson, and they took the book. Elliott's spirits
soared. He modified his once modest assessment of

his own work, now finding "a ring of scholarship about it that does not belong [to] the common field of sportsmen!"

The manuscript was soon set in type, but there was one small hold up. The publishers delayed printing *Carolina Sports* to accommodate a novel called *The Minister's Wedding*, by the reptilian Mrs. Stowe. Elliott waited humbly. "It is coarsely said of 'a barber's bench, that it suits all buttocks,'" he wrote, making light of the company he was keeping. When it was his book's turn he was happy with the results. "They print here so accurately," he beamed, comparing New York with Charleston. He had reason to hope. "I shall be surprised if it fails to make a noise," he exulted.

When you total the proceeds and pay back the printing costs, Elliott made sixty-two dollars in royalties from the 1859 edition of *Carolina Sports*—about what Herman Melville realized from *Moby-Dick*, and Henry David Thoreau from *Walden*. The country was moving to war and Elliott's stories, for all their drama and action, belonged to the past, but only to the recent past and not to a long-ago past that could give them antique value. Back home, devil-fishing had lost its novelty and was being ceremonialized to death. The Bishop came annually to bless the fishermen and a band came to play. Professional hunters supplying city butcher shops were rapidly thinning out the deer. Elliott's time was out, but no new era was in. "Our scepter . . . is departing from us," he wrote, referring to the Sea Islands'

domination of the long-staple cotton market, "and
finds lodgment in Florida." He vowed to explore the
cotton lands in Florida with an open mind to moving, but he never got around to it. The gentleman
cotton planter was obsolete; the planter who was
also a manufacturer had not yet come to be. "More
and more," the old time planter, gentleman or not,
was the "prey of monopolists and foreign agents."
His condition was "one of degrading dependence."

The problem was that planters could not control
the prices they received for their crops. They were
making money but losing influence, or so Elliott
believed. But it was the planters' dependence on a
different group of people that was their undoing. In
a letter posted the last week of August, 1862, Elliott
thanked General Johnson Hagood "for the use of a
detachment of cavalry . . . to arrest a stampede of
my Negroes from Oak Lawn—on their way to join
the Yankees." The use of soldiers to protect slave
property was justified, Elliott wrote, because "these
Negroes are the main source of our wealth, and the
product of their labor is the only fund which the
Confederate states can hope to support the war, and
pay the interest on our public debt, immense and
still accumulating." When slaves are allowed to run
away, two evils result. "Not only is a valuable pro-
ducer abstracted from us," he declared, revealing his
debt to Adam Smith and Thomas Malthus, but the
slave, "from the unprincipled conduct of our malig-
nant and unscrupulous foe, becomes a recruit in his

ranks, and is armed to cut the throat of his former master."

Things never came to that. Instead of seeking revenge, the freed slaves of the lowcountry sought land. Elliott's fear, however, was no doubt genuine; he had had words with the people he still considered his " Negroes," on his St. Helena Parish plantations, a month after the federal invasion of Port Royal in November, 1861. Finding them "insubordinate, refusing to work, and communicating with the enemy," he had asked for military help "to save property and restrain the Negroes." His request was refused, first by General Roswell Ripley, who claimed "no authority," and then by General Robert E. Lee who, fresh from his failure to hold western Virginia for the Confederacy, had been assigned to organize the defenses on the South Atlantic coast, but was having difficulty getting an accurate count of his force. Lee did agree to send enough soldiers to burn Elliott's cotton to keep it from falling into enemy hands. Ninety-seven thousand pounds of cotton in the seed, enough to make about one hundred bales, went up in smoke along with the cotton houses. At 1861 prices, the crop might have grossed thirty thousand dollars, which was a lot of money. Besides the cotton, Elliott's losses included the family house in Beaufort, three plantations and ninety-five slaves; twelve hundred bushels each of corn and potatoes, three hundred bushels of peas, one hundred and fifteen head of cattle, mules, cotton gins, boats, tools — virtually everything not kept at Oak Lawn or worn

on his back. The good fortune he had in persuading
General Hagood to send troops to Oak Lawn eight
months later—the Confederates still controlled the
Edisto, at least by day—resulted in only temporary
gains. Elliott punished the mutinous slaves by whip-
ping and handcuffing, and ordered two of the leaders
removed to Charleston to be sold. In his heart he
knew his property was doomed and he was already
thinking of the compensation he would be paid when
the war ended. His effort "to save something from
the wreck, which the invasion of the Yankees has
brought upon us," was cut short by his death from
"an inflamation of the intestines" in a Charleston
hotel; not a death in the saddle as he might have
wished, and not by the lights of his personal theology
one to be followed by eternal reward or damnation.

He had expressed the hope that his book would
"have a chance of being remembered for a few days
after my death." By that measure he achieved his
goal. The enemy could steal his corn, free his slaves,
and destroy his livestock, but they could not touch
his book. It was safe, on shelves everywhere. A copy
found its way to Thoreau, who was put off by Elliott's superior airs but enticed by his descriptions
of the lowcountry. He doubted Elliott's prophecy
that the people who were currently eating up the
deer would rally to save them from extermination
once the idea of protecting the wild had shed the
stigma of benefitting the rich. Thoreau and Elliott
could agree over whom the future belonged to: It
did not belong to men who thought that because

they owned the land they owned the deer too. It belonged, even if it was not wanted, to that masculine democracy which, in the half-baked form of the brotherhood of the hunt, Elliott had happily embraced.

Theodore Rosengarten

William Elliott's
CAROLINA SPORTS

BY

LAND AND WATER

" Do you know gentle reader, what a devil-fish is? . . . Imagine, then, a monster measuring from sixteen to twenty feet across the back, full three feet in depth, having powerful yet flexible flaps or wings, with which he drives himself furiously through the water, or vaults high into air: his feelers (commonly called horns) projecting several feet beyond his mouth."

CAROLINA SPORTS

DEVIL FISHING

Aʜ, Jean Ribault!—when, in 1562, thy bark, long tossed by tempests, found anchorage at last within the sheltered harbor of Port Royal, and thine eye rested, where no European eye had rested before, on the sweet woodland scenery that encompassed it about—what exulting thoughts must have been thine? When, gazing with pleasure on that broad expanse of water—so wide, as the memoir of your voyage, yet preserved to us, expresses it, "that the greatest ships of France, yea, the argosies of Venice, may enter there in safety"—and with admiration, at the gigantic pines that towered above the surrounding forests; while oaks, festooned with grey moss, or wreathed with yellow jessamine, bathed their magnificent limbs in the ocean spray—and the queenly magnolia flung the perfume of her white blossoms far over the murmuring waters—and herds of deer and buffalo browsed, unconscious of fear, on the luxuriant herbage—and birds of unknown plumage and unrivalled voice, fluttered and carolled among the trees—what pleasant fancies must have crowded upon thy mind! and who but must sympathize in thy emotions—thou pioneer and file-leader of the Huguenots?

The deep, too, had its attractions. "We took to our nets," says the same memoir, "and caught such a number of fish, that it was wonderful." Yet, half of these wonders was not guessed at by the ancient mariner, who first visited these waters. How few could they have seen, compared with the uncounted varieties that must have escaped the sweep of their nets! There was the golden bass; and the drum, with its mysterious, and, to a stranger, its startling sound; the porpoise, showing its back above the water; and the unseen and unsuspected tribes that thronged the depths below; the sting-ray, with its jagged spine; the saw-fish; the omnivorous shark; the mightiest, strangest, most formidable among them all for its strength, *the devil-fish*; then rarely seen, and deemed, even down to our own times, scarcely less fabulous than the Norwegian kraken!

But, do you know, gentle reader, what a devil-fish is? Perhaps you never saw one, even in a museum! Imagine, then, a monster measuring from sixteen to twenty feet across the back, full three feet in depth, having powerful yet flexible flaps or wings, with which he drives himself furiously through the water, or vaults high into air: his feelers (commonly called horns) projecting several feet beyond his mouth, and paddling all the small fry, that constitute his food, into that enormous receiver—and you have an idea, an imperfect one, of this curious fish, which annually, during the summer months, frequents our southern seacoast.

It is quite possible that, in the course of my sporting excursions, I have been brought more in contact with the devil-fish than any man living; and I trust, therefore, that I may escape the charge of presumption, in pretending to interest you with what I have remarked as peculiar in the habits of this fish, as well as with the method which I have successfully adopted in his capture. But, before we proceed thus far, I will ask your perusal of an essay, which, though it sometimes substitutes the conjectural for the positive, may nevertheless serve as an introduction to the less spirited, but more authentic sketches which are to follow.

There was a vague tradition in the family, that my grandfather had, on a certain occasion, sallied forth from his plantation (washed by the waters of Port Royal Sound) and captured one of these sea monsters. When a boy, I gathered from a garrulous old family servant, that an African, named "May," had been the spearsman on the occasion, and had actually leaped on the back of the fish, with his harpoon. From these hints, I composed the following devil-fish story, which was contributed to "Skinner's Sporting Magazine," and published in the fourth number of the first volume:

FISHING EXTRAORDINARY.

BEAUFORT, S. C.

To the Editor of the Sporting Magazine.

SIR: I am a hereditary sportsman, and inherit the tastes of my grandfather, as well as his lands.

Whoever has seen the beautiful bay on which they are seated (known on the map as Port Royal Sound), with its transparent waters stocked with a variety of sea-fish, while the islands, that gird it in, abound in deer and other game—will confess that it is a position well calculated to draw out whatever sporting propensities may have been implanted in us by nature.

Perceiving the relish with which some of your contributors talk of their capture of perch and trout of two pounds weight, and other fish of that calibre, I am tempted to give you an account of the sport enjoyed by my grandfather; and which bears the same relation to your lauded trout-fishing as a Bengal tiger hunt to a match at snipes.

There is a fish which annually visits the bay I have described, from May till August, but in smaller numbers than formerly. It is described by Linnæus as of the genus Ray, species dio-don. It is called by Dr. Mitchell (not without reason, from the bat-like structure of his flaps, or wings), "the vampire of the ocean." It is known with us as the "devil-fish." Its structure indicates great muscular power; it has long, angular wings, a capacious mouth—but the greatest singularity of its formation consists in its arms (or horns, as they are called), which extend on each side of the mouth, and serve as feeders. Its size, with us, is from fourteen to twenty-five feet, measured across the back transversely. Its longi-tudinal measurement is less. Valliant describes this fish as reaching the size of fifty feet, on the coast of Africa; but Valliant was a *traveller!* I am a sportsman merely, Mr. Editor, and claim no charter to exceed the truth. I must own, then, that the largest I have seen and measured was but eighteen feet across the back, from three to four feet thick, as it lay on the ground, had horns or feeders three feet in length, curiously articulated at the ends, so as to resemble the fingers of the human hand when clenched, and enjoyed an amplitude of mouth sufficient to admit of its receiving two aldermen abreast, had it relished such a quintessence of turtle!

It is the habit of this fish to ply these arms rapidly before its mouth while it swims, and to clasp with the utmost closeness and obstinacy whatever body it has once inclosed. In this way, the boats of fishermen have often been dragged from their moorings, and overset by the devil-fish having laid hold of the grapnel. It was in obeying this peculiarity of their nature, that a shoal of these fish, as they swept by in front of my grandfather's residence, would sometimes, at flood-tide, approach so near to the shore as to come in contact with the water fence, the firm posts of which they would clasp, and struggle to uptear, till they lashed the water into a foam with their powerful wings. This bold invasion of his landmarks my grandfather determined to resent. He launched his eight-oared barge, prepared his tackle, notified his neighbors of his plan, and waited patiently for the next appearance of his enemies.

2—C. S.

It was not many days before they reappeared, to renew their sports. He then manned his boat, and soon glided with muffled oars into the midst of the shoal. "May," said my grandfather to his favorite African slave, who acted as his harpooner, "look out for the leader, and strike a sure blow." "Let me 'lone for dat, massa," said "May," as, staff in hand, he planted his foot firmly on the bow of the barge. He stood there but a second, when, grasping his staff in both hands, he sprang into the air, and descended directly on the back of the largest devil-fish, giving the whole weight of his body to the force of the stroke! The weapon sunk deep into the body of the fish, and before he had tightened the rope, "May" had already swam to the boat, laid his hands on the gunwale, and been dragged on board by his fellow-blackies, who were delighted at his exploit.

The fish now dashed off furiously, with the barge in tow. The bugle sounded the concerted signal. The planters manned their boats to intercept the barge; and each boat, as it arrived, was lashed alongside of the barge, so that, shortly, a small fleet of boats was drawn swiftly along with the tide. They approached so near my grandfather's door, that he ordered a bowl of arrack punch to be prepared and sent on board. It soon arrived to refresh and exhilarate the sportsmen of the little squadron. To conclude my story, the fish was wearied out, drawn to the top of the water, speared to death, and, when landed on the beach, measured twenty feet across the back.

I suspect, Mr. Editor, if the truth were told, we have few sportsmen who would venture on the daring feat of the African "May." Had he belonged to the Saxon or Norman race, he had probably been knighted, and allowed to quarter on his shield the horns of the devil-fish, in token of his exploit! As it is, his praise had almost been unsung, "sacro quia caret vate."

Our modern sportsmen, far from attacking, are content to be let alone by these devil-fish. But two instances to the contrary have occurred within my recollection. The first eventuated in a sound ducking to the parties concerned: the last was more curious. A respectable planter, named Jones, who was remarkable for mechanical ingenuity, was in the habit of amusing himself, during the long days of the summer solstice, in constructing curious self-invented pieces of mechanism. Like a thousand others, he attempted the discovery of perpetual motion; at one time the mystery was detected in the shifting buckets of the self-tending Chinese wheel; at another, he had solved it by quicksilver, included in revolving wheels, applied so as to force down one side with such vigorous impulse as to drive up its opposite—after the manner in which our Yankee stage-drivers ascend their short hills. Still this fugacious problem escaped his grasp, and the unpropitiated monster, *friction*, like the malicious Genius in the Arabian tale, was ever thrusting in his Gorgon head, and converting motion into immobility.

It happened that Jones, while engaged in these inquiries, had gone to Beaufort in his small boat, manned with but two oars, and met, on his return to his plantation (which lay near the sea), two *devil-fish*, disporting themselves on the surface of the water, as innocently as if they had been *angel-fish*—now showing the dark hues of their broad backs, now thrusting up a horn, now vibrating a wing, and now impelling their enormous mass high in air by the lever of their powerful wings. Jones was a sportsman to the backbone; he cast a glance at the smallness of his boat, but it was a glance only; his eye rested on his bright harpoon, which lay invitingly at his side. He sprang forward, secured his line to the head of the boat, and darted his harpoon at the nearest of the sportive monsters. A violent fall, at full length, into the bottom of the boat, as it shot forward almost from beneath his feet, was the first indication he received that his aim had been good; and, casting upward his eyes, he beheld his little boat buried, as it were, in the waters, while the divided waves curled over it, but fell not (such was the rapidity of its motion) till they were fairly left astern. His oarsmen, like prudent fellows, had taken, through choice, the position which their master had adopted through necessity, and quietly prostrated themselves in the bottom of the boat, where they rightly supposed their situation was safest.

There is much that is pleasant in the excitation of violent motion! So thought Dr. Johnson. It is probable Jones would have added the proviso, "so long as the motion is under our regulation." It was not until some minutes had elapsed, that he had the presence of mind, or the power, to crawl from his recumbent posture, and occupy his appropriate seat at the stern, where, however, he soon settled himself, and enjoyed the whole luxury of his situation. The wind fanned his face, his hair streamed off at right angles from his head, and the water foamed furiously about the stem, as the boat, impelled by this more than Triton, darted through the waters with the speed of an arrow. And now he approached his home, and he rejoiced to see that several of his friends were assembled on the bluff to welcome his return. But what was their amazement, to behold and recognize Jones, seated upright in the stern of his boat, which seemed to fly through the waters without the aid of oar, oarsmen, sail or steam, or any apparent or visible impulsion. Amazement was their first emotion—joy was their second—and they shouted forth in triumph, as the thought suddenly flashed upon them, Jones has discovered *perpetual motion!* He shouted to them for assistance: "Man me a boat, my friends; hasten to my rescue." His voice, tremulous from excitement, or drowned by distance, never reached their ears. He waved his hat, and shouted again; hats waved in return, and a triumphant shout responded

from his friends—but no boat put off, no rescue
came! Que faut il faire? He had even to do, as
many a shrewd politician has done before him, lie
still, and watch some favorable turn of affairs.
"These violent motions," thought he, "must have an
end, and even devil-fish must tire. Friction, at least,
that has so often foiled me, now stands my friend."
The fish *did* pause at last, but not till the boat had
been hurried quite out of the harbor, and was
floating on the waters of the wide Atlantic. It was
then that our sportsman left his position at the stern,
where his weight had been necessary to preserve
the equipoise, and cut off, with his penknife, the line
which bound him to his formidable companion.
The oars had been lost overboard in the mêlée; the
sail, however, remained to waft him to his home.
But it was late at night when he arrived, exhausted
by excitement and fatigue, and explained to his
anxious friends the mystery of his unintelligible,
but fortunately for him, *not perpetual motion!*

PISCATOR.

To guard against misconstruction, I here repeat,
that a few leading incidents only of this story are
founded in truth, and that the rest is to be considered merely as a fancy-sketch; but, in making
this admission, I wish it at the same time distinctly
to be understood that in all the sketches that follow,
I shall confine myself strictly to the facts—that I
shall admit no fanciful embellishments—that I shall

report nothing which did not actually happen—and that the only license that I shall permit myself, will be that of selection. I shall not hesitate, of course, to reject and shut out such unmeaning incidents as could have no other effect than to clog and give tediousness to my narrative.

It was during the month of August, 1837, that, attended by my children, and by several friends, whose inducements were change of air and the benefit of sea-bathing, I made an excursion to Bay Point, a small summer settlement situated at the northeastern outlet of Port Royal Sound. There, for the first time, I witnessed the sporting of these sea monsters on the surface, and conceived the idea of taking them with the harpoon. How this purpose was carried into effect, will appear from the statement copied from the "Charleston Mercury," and dated 17th August, 1837.

BAY POINT, Aug. 17th, 1837.

To JOHN A. STUART, ESQ.:

I give you a hasty narrative of an affair which took place yesterday, between your humble servant and a devil-fish. It is due to you, as a native of this region, to whom all the localities are familiar— as a sportsman every inch, to whom such narratives will be a pleasure, and furthermore, as having in some sort provoked the adventure, by a recent boast of your own exploits in the fishing line.

On Saturday, the — August, taking advantage
of a short cessation in the storms that signalized
the week, I crossed from Bay Point to Hilton Head,
on a visit. In the course of the excursion, I saw
eight devil-fish sporting on the surface of the water.
One, directly in the track of my boat, as I spanked
away under a press of sail. He thrust up both wings
a foot above the surface, and kept them steadily
erect, as if to act for sails. I liked not the *cradle*
thus offered me, and veered the boat, so as just to
miss him. He never budged, and I passed so near,
as easily to have harpooned him, if the implements
had been at hand.

The devil-fish (in numbers thus unusual), had
doubtless run into the inlet to escape the gales; for
from repeated observations, I am persuaded that fish
are provided with an instinct, by which they are
forewarned of convulsions in their proper element.

The sight of these fish disturbed my rest, and I
felt uncomfortable, until I found myself planning
an attack and providing myself with the needful
apparatus. A harpoon, two inches wide in the barb,
between two and three feet in the shank (a regular
whaler), was turned out from the workshop of Mr.
Mickler. Forty fathoms of half-inch rope were
purchased and stretched. To one end the harpoon
was firmly attached; the other, passing through a
hole cut in the bottom of a tub, in which the rope
was carefully coiled, was to be fastened to the forecastle. A six-oared boat was inspected, new

thwarted, and new thole-pinned; and a clete nailed firmly on the forecastle to support the right foot of the harpooner. A day was fixed, and friends and sportsmen were invited to repair to the field of action; but the weather was unpropitious, and but two boats appeared.

At six o'clock on Wednesday, the 16th August, we started from Bay Point on our cruise for devil-fish. In my boat, manned by six oarsmen and a steersman, I was accompanied by my son, a youth under eighteen. In the second boat were G. P. E., and W. C., Esqrs., with a crew of four men. The armament of the larger consisted, besides the harpoon, of a lance, hatchet, and rifle; that of the smaller boat, was two bayonets fixed in long staves (the line which was to have been rigged to a second harpoon, having been swept away with a sharp hook attached, by an overwhelming spring tide the night before). We stretched away before a fresh north-easter, for the Bay gall on Hilton Head, and then struck sail and made all snug for action. Masts, sails, awnings, were all stowed away in the bottom of the boat, the anchor with its rope, was transferred to the platform for *trim*, and that nothing should interfere with our running gear. Here a large shoal of porpoises came plunging about us; the harpoon was poised, but none came within striking distance; and after being tantalized by this show of unexpected sport, a rifle shot among them sent them booming off, and left us leisure to pursue our proper game.

We rowed slowly along between the Bay gall breaker and the shore, on the early ebb, expecting to meet the devil-fish on their return from Skull Creek, the scene of their high water gambols. The smaller boat, with outspread sails, stretched off and on, traversing the same region, but on different lines. No fish were seen. We advanced in front of Mrs. E.'s avenue, and took another survey, and thus slowly extended the cruise to Skull Creek, while our consort stretched away as far as Pinckney's Island. The ebb was half spent, and we began to despair. I landed on the beach at Hilton Head, yet kept the boat afloat, and two hands on the lookout. Before a quarter of an hour had elapsed, "There," cried our lookout man. I followed the direction of his hand—it pointed to Skull Creek channel, and I saw the wing of the fish two feet above water. There was no mistaking it—it was a devil-fish. One shout summons the crew to their posts—the red flag is raised to signal our consort—the oarsmen spring to their oars—and we dashed furiously onward in the direction in which we had seen him. Once again before we had accomplished the distance, he appeared a moment on the surface.

The place of harpooner I had not the generosity to yield to any one; so I planted myself on the forecastle, my left leg advanced, my right supported by the clete, my harpoon poised, and three fathoms of rope lying loose on the thwart behind me. The interest of the moment was intense; my heart throbbed audibly, and I scarcely breathed, while expecting him to emerge from the spot yet rippled by his wake. The water was ten fathoms deep, but so turbid that you could not see six inches beneath the surface. We had small chance of striking him while his visits to the surface were so sudden and so brief. "There he is behind us!" "Starn all"— and our oarsmen, as before instructed, backed with all their might. Before we reached the spot he was gone; but soon reappeared on our right, whisking round us with great velocity, and with a movement singularly eccentric. He crossed the bow—his wing only is visible—on which side is his body? I hurled down my harpoon with all my force. After the lapse of a few seconds, the staff came bounding up from below, to show me that I had missed. In the twinkling of an eye, the fish flung himself on his back, darted under the boat, and showed himself at the stern, *belly up*. Tom clapped his unarmed hands with disappointment as the fish swept by him where he stood on the platform, so near that he might have pierced him with a sword! And now the fish came wantoning about us—taking no note of our presence, circling round us, with amazing rapidity, yet showing nothing but the tip of his wing. We dashed at him whenever he appeared, but he changed position so quickly, that we were always too late. Suddenly his broad black back was lifted above the water directly before our bow. "Forward!" the oarsmen bend to the stroke, but

before we could gain our distance, his tail flies up,
and he is plunging downward for his depths. I
could not resist—I pitched my harpoon, from the
distance of full thirty feet. It went whizzing
through the air, and cleaved the water just beneath
the spot where the fish had disappeared. My companions in our consort (who had now approached
within fifty yards) observed the staff quiver for a
second before it disappeared beneath the surface of
the water. This was unobserved by myself, and I
was drawing in my line to prepare for a new throw,
when ho! the line stopped short! "Is it possible? I
have him—the devil-fish is struck!" Out flies the
line from the bow—a joyful shout bursts from our
crew—our consort is lashed to our stern—E. and C.
spring aboard—and here we go! driven by this most
diabolical of locomotives.

Thirty fathoms are run out, and I venture a turn
round the stem. The harpoon holds, and he leads
gallantly off for Middle Bank—the two boats in
tow. He pushed dead in the eye of a stiff north-
easter. His motion is not so rapid as we expected,
but regular and business-like—reminding one of the
motion of a canal boat drawn by a team of stout
horses. On Middle Bank he approached the surface—the rifle is caught up, but soon laid aside as
useless, for no vulnerable part appeared. We then
drew upon the line, that we might force him to the
surface and spear him—I soon found *that* was no
fun. "Tom, don't you want to play a devil-fish?

I have enough to last me for an hour, so here's my place, if you desire it." Behold me now reclined on the stern seat, taking breath after my pull, and lifting my umbrella to repel the heat of the sun. It was very pleasant to see the woods of Hilton Head recede, and the hammocks of Paris Island grow into distinctness, as we moved along under this novel, and *yet unpatented* impelling power! "You will find this melon refreshing, friends! at twelve o'clock, let us take a glass of wine to our success. Tom, why don't you pull him up?" Tom held up his hands, from which the gloves had been stripped clean by the friction of the rope. "We'll put three men to the line and bouse on him." He comes! George seizes the lance, but the devil-fish stops ten feet below the surface, and can't be coaxed nearer. George sinks his long staff in the direction of the line, feels the fish, and plunges the lance into him. It is flung out of his body, and almost out of the hand of the spearsman, by the convulsive muscular effort of the fish. When drawn up, the iron was found bent like a reaping hook, and the staff broken in the socket. The fish now quickened his speed, and made across Daws' Channel for Paris Bank.

"Just where we would have you, my old boy— when we get you near Bay Point Beach, it will be so convenient to land you!" He seems to gather velocity as he goes; he gets used to his harness; points for Station Creek, taking the regular steam-

boat track. As soon as he gains the deep channel,
he turns for Bay Point. "Now, then, another trial—
a bouse on him." Three fellows are set to the rope—
his wing appears—C—— aims his bayonet, and
plunges it deep into his body—another shudder of
the fish, and the bayonet snaps short off at the eye—
the blade remains buried in his body. "Now for it,
George!" *His* bayonet is driven in, and, at the
second blow, *that* is snapped off in the blade. Here
we are unweaponed! our rifle and hatchet useless,
our other implements broken! "Give him rope,
boys, until we haul off and repair damages." At
every blow we had dealt him, his power seemed to
have increased, and he now swept down for Egg
Bank, with a speed that looked ominous. "Out
oars, boys, and pull against him." The tide was
now flood—the wind still fresh, had shifted to the
east: six oars were put out and pulled lustily against
him, yet he carried us rapidly seaward, against all
these impeding forces. He seemed to suck in fresh
vigor from the ocean water. George meanwhile was
refitting the broken implements; the lance was fixed
in a new staff, and secured by a tie of triple drum
line; the broken blade of the bayonet was fixed on
another staff. Egg Bank was now but one hundred
yards to our left. "Row him ashore, boys." The
devil-fish refused, and drew the whole concern in the
opposite direction. "Force him, then, to the surface." He popped up unexpectedly under the bow,
lifted one wing four feet in the air, and bringing it

suddenly down, swept off every oar from the starboard side of the boat; they were not broken, but
wrenched out of the hands of the oarsmen as by an
electric shock. One man was knocked beneath the
thwarts by the rebound of an oar, and was laid
almost speechless on the platform—quite *hors de
combat*. Fresh hands are brought from the smaller
boat; the fish now leads off with thirty fathoms of
rope—he steers for Joyner's Bank. Bay Point
recedes, Egg Bank disappears, Chaplin's Island lies
behind us, and Hilton Head again approaches, but
it is the *eastern face* of the island that now presents
itself. The breakers of the Gaskin Bank begin to
loom in our horizon, and *this* is done against wind,
tide and oar! A doubt of capturing the fish began
now to steal over our minds, and show itself in our
faces; our means of assailing so powerful an antag-
onist, were too inadequate; nothing remained but
to bouse on him once more, and endeavor to dispatch
him with the weapons that remained to us. Three
fresh hands took the rope, and after giving him
a long run to weary him to the uttermost, we succeeded in drawing him to the surface. He lay on
his back without motion—and we looked on victory
as certain. The socket of the harpoon appeared
sticking out, from the *belly* of the fish: the whole
shank was buried in his body. We saw neither tail
nor head, nor horns, nor wings—nothing but an
unsightly white mass, undistinguished by member
or feature. After a moment's pause, to single out

some spot for a mortal blow, I plunged the lance,
socket and all, into the centre of this white mass.
The negroes who held the line of the harpoon took
a turn round the gunwale, to prevent its slipping.
The boat lurched with the swell of the sea—and
the moment the dead weight of the fish, unsupported
by the water, was felt, the harpoon tore out!   An
instant before, I saw it driven to the socket in the
body of the fish, the next, it was held up in the air
in the hands of the negro, bent like a scythe.   There
was time, if there had been presence of mind, to
plunge it anew into the fish, which floated a second
or two on the surface.   The moment was lost!   I
will not attempt to describe the bitter disappointment that pervaded the party.   For a moment, only,
a faint hope revived; my lance, secured by a cord,
was still in his body—it might hold him!   "Clear
my line, boys!"   Alas! the weight of the fish is too
much for my tackle—the line flies through my hand
—is checked—the socket of the lance is drawn
through the orifice by which it entered—*and the
fish is gone!*   We spoke not a word, but set our sails,
and returned to the beach at Bay Point.   We felt
like mariners, who, after a hard conflict, had sunk
a gallant adversary at sea—yet saved not a single
trophy from the wreck to serve as a memorial of
their exploit.

Yet, keenly as we felt our disappointment, there
is not one of us who would willingly have been
elsewhere—and the pleasurable excitement of our

three hours' run, will be remembered to the end of our lives.

We struck the fish at eleven o'clock, a mile below Skull Creek, and lost him at two, near the tail of Joyner's Bank, four miles below Bay Point. His course was first northeast, then southeast, then south by east. The direct run, taking no note of his occasional deviations, was fifteen miles. He was struck in the belly, from which it would appear he was executing a somersault, when reached by the harpoon. The harpoon must have passed through to his back, or it could not have resisted the tremendous pressure applied for three hours. It entered probably not far from the insertion of the tail, and passed out near the back bone, for the rapidity of his motion was striking before he was harpooned, but afterward he seemed to effect more by gravity than by velocity. The entire fish was at no time seen—his size must be matter of conjecture: fourteen feet across the back, I think no extravagant calculation. How much gratified should we be if he should float ashore and terminate these conjectures, for we cannot doubt but that he has been *killed*, though not *captured*.

Our oarsman, injured in the affray, has been bled, and is doing well—so that nothing remains to mar our satisfaction, but the loss of our fish. But stop, Mr. Editor—while I am penning this line, a devil-fish is flouncing along the shore, under my very nose, as if in bravado. By the ghost of *Lignum vitæ*, I

will try another turn with him as soon as my tackle
can be repaired!

PISCATOR.

The threat with which this narrative concluded
was soon carried into execution. On the 25th day
of August, 1837, three boats appeared at the rendezvous at Bay Point, fully equipped for the sport, and
commenced a cruise, full of exciting incident, and,
as will appear in the sequel, eminently successful.
In my own boat, I was accompanied by Edmund
Rhett, Esq., and by my son, Thos. R. S. Elliott, and
cousin, Jas. H. Elliott—mere youths, but not on that
account the less eager for the sport. In the next
boat were G. P. Elliott, Wm. Cuthbert, John G.
Barnwell, and Robt. W. Barnwell, Esqrs. The
third boat was occupied by Ed. B. Means and William Jenkins, youths likewise, and amateur observers
rather than actors in the scene. I did not write or
publish any account of this day's adventure, at the
time, for several reasons. One was that I was
known under my assumed signature of "Piscator,"
the mask was no longer a disguise; and I feared
that even a truthful narrative of adventures, in
which I bore so large a part, might be construed
into an offensive egotism; another was that two
several versions were published, by others who were
present, and eye-witnesses of the facts they nar-
rated. The first was published in the "Charleston
Mercury," in the form of a letter, dated Beaufort,

Sept. 2d, 1837; and the second appeared in the April
number of the "Southern Literary Journal," year
1838, and page 267. The reader, who will discover
with what spirited touches and masterly strokes this
last named article abounds, will readily excuse me
for adopting so large a portion of it, instead of
writing out the story *de novo.*

"DEVIL FISHING.

"BEAUFORT, S. C.

"After all, there is no sport the world over, like the fisherman's.   What of your horse-racing, theatre-gazing, or
tripping it down, of a hot summer's night, to the clatter of
noteless pianos, split clarionets, cold iron triangles, and
crazy tambourines? No! Give me a tight boat, clean tackle,
a few jolly friends, and a warm, pleasant sky, and adieu,
ladies and gentlemen, to your dry-land pastimes, as you
have no zest for what are far richer, I assure you, if they
are more dearly bought.   Pardon me, if I can't dance to
your piping—the fashion of the thing is gone—the soul that
once animated it is dead, and is to have, for *us*, no resur-
rection.

"Those who know anything of our coast, will recollect
the beautiful frith called the Broad River, which comes up
at about latitude 32° between Hilton Head and Jenkins'
Island, for some miles into the interior; its margin at a
distance fringed with tall green wood, descending to the
water's edge, and varied here and there by clusters of white
houses grouping in the prospect like fleets of sail at anchor,
or by the glitter of a tributary river flowing down from
the rich inlands beyond, or perhaps by an occasional glimpse
of a cool vista, leading the eye up to some cheerful retreat
of hospitable wealth.   All this region had been the theatre
of many a revolutionary adventure, not yet passed from the
memories of the living.   But of late years, Broad River was
famous chiefly for its fine fishing.   Drum in the spring, bass

in autumn, and so on through the seasons. But a new object
was now drawing the eyes of the curious. A nondescript
creature, unlike anything before heard of in the heavens
above, or the earth beneath, had been seen twirling his
giant form, bat-like, along the shores, now protruding his
broad flaps in graceful curves above the surface and now
starting with the nimbleness of a silver-fish, his full length
into the air, and returning in a cloud of spray and foam
into his native depths. Some called it the vampire, others
the devil-fish, and not a few, shaking their heads signifi-
cantly, wished to know how it came to pass, that some *one*
(nameless to 'ears polite') had so much more countenance in
these parts than formerly. Marvellous, too, were the tales
of his doings in Broad River. He once took up the anchor
of an eight-oared boat, without the least provocation, and
made off to sea with it, in spite of the outcries and struggles
of the occupants, whom he would undoubtedly have left to
the care of Providence among the breakers, but for the
arrival of friends just in time to save the shivering adventurers from the gripe of their adversary. It was also said,
on the very best authority, that a fisherman once ran his
boat aground on

   " 'Him haply slumbering on the Norway foam,'

and was about 'casting anchor on his scaly rind,' 'deem-
ing him some island,' when dash went the oars, and away
bounced the insulted monster, leaving the 'night-foundered
skiff' tilting and trembling like a nut-shell in his wake.
Credat Judaeus Appella. All this, however, moved men
not a little. No one dared to approach him in his slum-
ber, or to disturb his solitary gambols over the banks, until
within a week or so, when he was harpooned outright in
Skull Creek channel, as he was 'taking his pleasure' there,
and after some hours of hot pursuit, escaped only by the
barbs of the weapon tearing out of his body in the very
crisis of complete conquest. But 'Piscator' was there; what
wonder if the shaft took effect which was wielded by such
a hand!

 "But *paulo majora canamus.* The devil-fish might be
taken; and we resolved to delay the adventure not a

moment. On the morning of the 25th of August, three boats might be descried moving briskly from the Bay Point shore across Broad River, two of them furnished each with a harpoon, lances, cordage, etc., manned by a party of high spirits, eager for the rapture of this new but perilous pastime. A number of amateurs had taken passage in the third boat, which was to lag behind, with a view to picking up whatever fell overboard from its companions in the confusion of the scuffle, on condition of being allowed to be always in a situation to escape seasonably from danger. The sun was already high; but a light breeze which came in from the sea relieved the intensity of its rays, which descended on our heads through a bright, liquid sky. The blubber, taking advantage of the flood, were seen in troops at our side, throbbing their bright, silky forms toward the banks up the river. A shark now and then shot his fin across our track, as he dashed into a shoal of fry, startling the whole glittering tribe into the air; while over our heads the sea-gull wended his easy flight, now swooping gracefully to the surface and then rising on the wind with his dreary clack, reminding one of the cry of a doomed spirit.

"We were now moving leisurely along the Hilton Head shore, looking out for our foe in one of his old haunts, about a large trunk which rose black with age and barnacles, some ten or fifteen feet above water. Not a sign of him was discovered. We looked in the direction of Skull Creek, but he was obviously not there, for the surface was as quiet as if he had never ruffled it. A glance toward the sea at our backs gave us as little satisfaction. In the meantime, it was evident from the water-marks on our left, that the flood was far advanced, and that the bank would soon be too deep to reach him if he came fishing upon it. Impatience was visible in every countenance.

"'The day is fine enough,' said P.; 'they ought to be hereabouts, for the boys saw them only yesterday.'

"'I have my doubts,' said another, 'as to everything the rogues tell us, especially if a devil-fish is in the matter. You know their superstition.'

" 'Ah, gentlemen,' exclaimed a third, rising from his seat, and gaping with ennui, 'this comes of taking things too late; you should have followed my advice, and have come out earlier. As it is, I see we shall have no sport.'

" 'Look on your right!' shouted a voice from the other boat.

"The whole party were, in an instant, on their feet. There they were to be sure. One, two, three, only a few hundred yards from us, rioting and tumbling fantastically over each other's wakes.

" 'Where is the harpoon?'—'the rifle!'—'the rifle!' exclaimed several voices at once.

" 'Gentlemen, do be quiet,' said P., as he leaped on the forecastle, catching up at the same time the harpoon, which lay on a coil of rope ready for use. 'I have seen some of this service before: pray, go aft, and let me have a clear swing. By the way, Tom, my son, hold up that umbrella— there is no merit in spoiling your face unnecessarily. Why will you throw away Dr. Muhlenburg's instructions in this manner? Now, boys, to your oars.'

"A few brisk strokes brought us in the midst of the play-ground of the devil-fish, over a bank two or three fathoms deep. No part of their bodies was, however, to be seen; nothing but their broad, dingy flaps, their coppered edges glancing to the sun, as they rose and sunk in graceful parabolas through the turbid brine. All besides was dark: it was not possible to know where to strike. Their motions, too, were so rapid and disorderly, and withal transiently perceptible, that it required our utmost efforts to shift our boat into available positions. But our *facile princeps*—the master-spirit of fishermen—was at the bow. An opportunity at last offered, and away went the harpoon, and, in a twink-ling, the smallest fish disappeared: he had felt the touch of its keen edge, and instantly took fright. Another followed his example, leaving the bank in possession of one, who now seemed concerned only to show how swiftly and nimbly he could acquit himself. Instead of emerging, as before, at intervals of a few yards, he took reaches of twenty or thirty at a time—not one of them on the same line with another—

gyrating, as he went, into the most fantastic attitudes. At
last, the surface was all quiet; every one held his breath.
A heavy whirl appeared at the head of the boat—what did
it mean? But Piscator knew, and the harpoon once more
took flight, and descending five or six feet into the water,
stood quivering there for a moment, and then vanished with
the velocity of light.

"'Habet!' shouted a sort of linguist (who was always
boring us with his scrap Latin, to make amends, it was
supposed, for his bad English), as he grasped the line and
huzzaed, until the shore resounded with the music of his
lungs. And it was but too true. The devil-fish, after his
other frolics, had vaulted entirely on his back, and came
floating on the tide, stomach upward; his white form
reflected along the surface for several yards. A mark so
palpable could hardly escape the stroke of our weapon: it
entered his abdomen about the middle, and cut its way
right down nearly three feet into his vitals. The line was
clear for him to the extent of thirty fathoms; but, after
running fifteen or twenty, he went plump to the bottom,
defying every effort at removal. At length he gave way,
and after much tugging rose logishly to the top—but day-
light inspired him with new strength, and he bounded off
again at the height of his speed. Our man of particles was
now in a sore dilemma. This 'learned Theban' had been
rude enough to throw the line so carelessly about his feet,
that there was every prospect of his being speedily caught
in its flying tangles, and ducked soundly for his pains.
What was he to do? A leap or two heavenward showed
that would not answer; so, clearing the forecastle at a
bound, he lit in the body of the boat, with no other harm
done than some commotion among the rigging, a cry of
wonderment from the oarsmen, and sundry ejaculations of
thanksgiving to Providence from himself. The line now
slacked, and the devil-fish was obviously giving out. He
yielded freely to the hand, and, as the last scene in the
drama approached, the boats gathered around to witness his
expiring struggles. The line swayed, and up he rose, his

huge goggles peering out upon us, while his antennæ dangled heavily about, in token of the extremest exhaustion. One more effort at escape followed; but it was too late—the lances were ready, and soon consummated the work of death; after which, we all joined in merry procession toward the shore. We drew the devil-fish on the sands, and found him, on measurement, to be fifteen feet in width."

Here, then, we have captured our devil-fish. He lies stranded on the beach of Hilton Head Island, at the foot of the Queen's Oak. This monster, whose existence even was doubted—whose capture was matter of vague tradition—who had not been seen and touched by the *two* preceding generations of men, to say the least—was here before us in his proper proportions, palpable to sight, and trodden beneath our feet! We congratulate each other on our success, and then betake ourselves to an examination of what was curious or striking in his conformation. We note with lively surprise his protruding eyes, his projecting horns, his capacious mouth, and his complicated machinery for respiration. We note, too, that like the great ones of the earth, he is attended by a band of parasites, which, unlike their prototypes of this earth, remain attached to their patrons *after they are stranded*. The pilot-fish, or sucking-fish (properly "remora"), which followed him into shoal water, adhered so closely after he was aground, that several suffered themselves to be taken by the hand.

Having satisfied our own curiosity, our next thought was to satisfy that of our friends; and we

hastened to dispatch our fish to Bay Point and
Beaufort. Transferring to our boat the two amateurs who occupied the tender, we supplied her
with our anchors in addition to her own, to secure
her against being drifted to sea, and saw her fairly
off, impelled by sail and oar, with the devil-fish in
tow. Then, turning to examine our tackle, we found
it terribly in disrepair; the rope knotted and tangled,
the staff splintered, the harpoon bent like a reaping-
hook! We had scarcely dispatched it by a runner
to a neighboring smith, to be set in order, when a
shoal of fish were seen sporting in the channel
abreast of us! "Have at them," said our companions in the second boat, as their oarsmen sprang
to the oars. "Wait for us—let us still cruise in
company," cried we, in turn. We might have saved
our breath—our companions did not heed us—the
temptation was too strong for weak mortality, and
we saw them bounding on confidently to the game,
of which we were condemned to remain but the
passive and distant spectators. We followed them
with our eyes, until we beheld our consort in the
midst of a shoal, which kept wantoning about them.
The harpoon is thrown, the boat darts forward, and
a black and unsightly object of immense bulk vaults
into the air, at the head of the boat—then plunges
into the depths below, and drags the boat rapidly
in its wake. Meantime we are fuming with
impatience, and while our runner hurries to us
with our harpoon, we scarcely allow ourselves time

to adjust it to the staff, before we push off from shore—so fearful were we that we should lose *our share* of the sport. There was no loitering by the way, and we soon come within hail. "What cheer, comrades? Do you need our help?" "Oh, by no means—*we* can manage him." "Very well, then, we look out for ourselves;" and we dashed at a fish that was showing himself at intervals astern of the other boat. Again my foot is on the fore-castle—again the harpoon is poised—and, before five minutes have elapsed, the barb is planted in him, and we are drawn over the placid water in nearly the same course with our consort.

To the mere lover of the picturesque, the scene which now presented itself must have been full of interest; but to every one possessed of the true spirit of a sportsman, it must have been as exciting as it was novel! The winds were hushed, and the wide expanse of water on which we floated was smooth as a mirror. The tender, with her devil-fish in tow, was before us. The tide, still flood, was drifting her up the river, and out of her desired course. See! she has let go her anchors, hauled her fish close up under her stern, and the boatmen are beating off with their oars the sharks, that, having scented the blood, as it flowed from many a ghastly wound, can scarcely be deterred by blows from gorging themselves on the immense but life-less mass! Further from shore glides the Sea-Gull—the first energies of the monster fish that impels her have apparently been tamed down, and she tacks across the channel, like a barge beating to windward! Jests, merriment and laughter are rife on board of her; and the mirthful echoes are borne to us over the still waters. Behind her is our own boat—whilom the Cotton-Plant, but baptized anew, after her capture of two hours since—"The Devil-Fish;" and her crew, with less noise, but not with less zest, are enjoying the luxury of the scene! *Three boats, each with a devil-fish!* Such are the compensations, ye sportsmen who inhabit more genial climes! which we find, *or make for ourselves*, in latitude 32°, under our blazing sky, when the sun is peering down vertically upon our heads by day, and the pestilence is abroad by night!

The fish, meantime, which we had struck, was moving sluggishly through the water. He had never drawn out half the rope, and seemed as if he did not feel, or else disdained the harpoon which was fastened in him; when suddenly he darted off at right angles with his former course. "Hillo there! give him more rope! How furiously he goes! Surely the sharks have scented him, too, for he rushes on like a stricken buffalo chased by a gang of prairie wolves. Rope! give him rope! Head the boat round! helm down! pull, starboard oar!" All in vain: the forty fathoms are out—she broaches to broadside—something must give way, or we capsize! The boat groans in every timber—the gunwale already kisses the wave—when shweep!

the harpoon fairly bounds out of the fish (which the severity of the strain had drawn to the surface), and flies into the air, as if shot from some submarine swivel! The boat rocks fearfully from side to side, then settles again on an even keel! The risk and the sport are over at the same instant! and we draw in our harpoon, which was twisted into all manner of unserviceable shapes, and row a second time to the shore to have it repaired. We landed at Mrs. Elliott's plantation, and refreshed ourselves with fruits and melons, until our purpose was effected; when we sallied forth once more in quest of sport. The harpoon was now transferred to the hands of the younger sportsmen; but the fish had grown shy, showed themselves but seldom, and then for so short a time, that before we could succeed in striking another, our attention was drawn off in a new direction. We looked for our consort, and saw her several miles to the east. The sea-breeze had sprung up—her sails were set, but she was dragged with ominous speed in a direction opposite to her intended course. "Vestigia nulla retrorsum"—stern foremost, like the beeves of Cacus, was she wending her way to the den of the devil-fish. Possibly there is less merriment on board of her than when we parted company! Possibly they begin to comprehend the advantage of a cruise in company! No matter! we must intercept her, before she is carried out to sea.

I here resume the narrative from the "Literary Journal," which I have interrupted by these remarks:

"One or two hours passed, and our friends had not yet made any progress toward the capture of their devil-fish. They were, in truth, quite at his mercy. In the first instance, he took them over to Paris Island Bank. He then entered the Beaufort River, where, after several turns and returns, as if hesitating what to do, he crossed over to the St. Helena shore, and coasted along that, until, falling into the Bay Point channel, he took a steady course for the ocean. All their efforts to bring him within reach of the lances were fruitless: the oars were out, the sails all set, and a smacking breeze blowing right over the bar: it was all in vain. Nothing either delayed or diverted his progress. Having no banks now in his way, it was obvious that his speed was becoming greater every moment. Very little of the day, moreover, remained. The sun was just above the mass of green woods in the west, sinking majestically into an amphitheatre of bright clouds, which seemed to heap about him in glorious homage to his departing rays. Far down in the opposite direction the white sails of our companion might be seen rolling and bending before the wind, as she went helplessly on toward the breakers. Yet, *we* were several miles up the river! Could we overtake them? Was it not too late? However, not a moment was to be lost. Every oarlock was filled—every hand grasped an oar—every sinew strained to the animating task. The devil-fish, after all, was to be slain by us! As we approached, the report of a gun came booming toward us, giving notice of another device of our friends to check his course. He had at last risen to the surface, and the effect of buckshot was tried upon him. But if he was touched it served no other purpose than to quicken his speed. We threw ourselves on the course of the other boat, some forty or fifty yards ahead.

" 'Where is the devil-fish?' shouted P.

"A sign with the hand directed us some distance beyond, where we saw indistinctly the wings of the devil-fish, shooting alternately out to the height of a foot or more. We were soon over him; but, with all his skill, P. could not reach his body. Stroke after stroke failed. The rocking of the boat, and the exhaustion of the oarsmen, under their constant exertions to keep up with him, made things still worse. Was he to escape from us after all? 'Strike, sir, for the black side of his wing;' but the advice was not wanted, for the harpoon was already deep in him. As before, the devil-fish now went directly for the bottom; but we were in the channel, and that resource could not avail him. He played about for some time, but we finally succeeded in bringing him up within six feet of us, where we pierced him with our lances until life was gone. But no force could lift him higher. By this time another boat had come from the Point to our aid, which, with the two we had already, it was thought, would be quite sufficient to take our fish ashore. The sails were set, and the oars put out to the number of eighteen; the wind, too, was as fair as could be wished—still there was no headway. The devil-fish was, indeed, unmanageable; and but for the force of the wind counteracting the outward tendencies of the tide, we must have been inevitably swept to sea, or have cut him loose to save ourselves. Darkness, in the meantime, had set in. The night was advancing, and we were yet almost stationary. Our friends on shore, alarmed at our situation, set up lights for us, which, owing to their dispersion, did more to confound than guide us. The stars came out; but nothing seemed to break the general darkness except the agitation of the oars in the water and the rolling of the devil-fish, as he now and then emerged on a bed of fire to the surface. At 9 o'clock we ran aground upon a shoal, which proved to be Egg Bank. We were now at a stand, and a council was called. It was impossible to get the devil-fish over the bank, for the tide was not high enough; and the roar of the breakers behind us, added to the rising of the wind, informed us too plainly that we could not safely remain where we were. Perhaps the devil-fish might be anchored: but no anchor was to be had; no buoy—not even a barrel by which he might be designated the next morning. The resource left us was a hard one; but there was no choice—we must abandon him—we could do no more. Before taking leave of him, however, we drew him up into three feet water.

> " 'Jacet ingens littore truncus
> —— et *sine nomine* corpus.'

"There he lay, extending twenty feet by the wings, and his other parts in proportion; and the waves rippling in pearly heaps around his black form, which stood eight feet in diameter above the water. We cut out our harpoons, pushed our boats through a neighboring swash, and, in a few moments, found ourselves surrounded by the welcoming eyes of beauty.

"R."

It is not to be inferred, from the concluding passage of the narrative just quoted, that the fish was eight feet in depth—but merely that, grounding in three feet water, such was his depth that a portion of his back, equal to eight feet in diameter, was still left above water. I know not that I ever witnessed anything more strikingly picturesque, than the appearance of the devil-fish just before he stranded. The night was dark—the sea brilliantly luminous—the breakers were roaring a short distance from us, and the ground-swell that at intervals lifted us up, admonished us that we were in shoal water. Looking behind us we beheld the devil-fish, which we had in tow, mounted upon the crest of an advancing wave. His wings outspread

—his dark outline distinctly marked, and separated from the surrounding waters by a "starry belt" of phosphoric fire—he seemed to our excited imaginations like some monster vampire, hovering above our heads, and threatening to crush us beneath his wings! There was scarcely time for apprehension, however, before he grounded, and that in water sufficiently deep to keep our boats afloat.

To leap into the sea—to mount his back in triumph, and shout a wild huzza! were impulses that we all felt and obeyed. Our next thought was to secure our retreat to the shore. We were embayed among the flats: the wind was rising—the tide falling. If we grounded, and were caught in that situation by the next flood, our boats would be beaten to pieces, and we should have but a small chance for our lives. The manner of our extrication has been already told.

The friends who came to our assistance from Bay Point, were ——— and ———, Esqrs., sportsmen of the conservative order, who had a proper respect for their lives! They left us at nightfall, offering to make fires which might guide us to the shore— executing, I must admit, a masterly retreat, under cover of this fire. The fire was not without its use; and had the stars been obscured, would have been indispensable to our safety. I am far from reflecting on these gentlemen. I think they did what was perfectly consistent with their position. *They* had not struck the fish, and were bound by no point of honor, to lie by an unmanageable prize, and encounter the hazards of a night adventure among the breakers.

The results of this day's sport, I need hardly say, were exceedingly grateful. We had seen the fish—had measured strength with them—*and captured two!* We had led the way in a new and exciting sport. We had done what none had done before, and what few might hope to exceed. We might now retire from the scene, and, hanging up our battered harpoons among the trophies of our humble rostral column, amuse our children with the histories that belonged to them.

———

Several years elapsed before I renewed my attempts against the devil-fish. I was otherwise occupied—and the scouts that I sometimes sent, to observe whether the fish were there, reported "that they did not see them"—so that I inferred (what I now believe to be incorrect) that their visits to the coast were but occasional. In the year 1843, however, I passed the month of July at Bay Point, and determined to investigate for myself. I found them in abundance, and enjoyed excellent sport, throughout that and the succeeding month, chiefly in company with Wm. Henry Mongin, Esq., of Dawfuskie, whose equipments were of the first order. On one day we captured a fish apiece. In the course

4—C. S.

of the season, I harpooned sixteen with my own
hand, but succeeded in landing but seven. I lost
many by striking them with the lance, before a
second harpoon had been planted; a practice that
I thenceforward abandoned. The largest fish that
I brought to the shore this season, measured seventeen feet six inches across—drew me quite out to sea
—and resisted with so much energy, that we were
seven hours and a half, after striking him, before
we could effect a landing, though several boats lent
us their assistance. I published an account of but
one of my adventures of this season; it is found
in the columns of the "Charleston Courier," 3d
August, 1843. The young gentleman that accompanied me, was Thomas M. Rhett, then a cadet of
West Point. The party who assisted in landing the
prize, were Edward B. Means, and Haskell Rhett,
Esqrs. I proceed with the narrative.

DEVIL FISHING.

BAY POINT, July, 1843.

You ask me for a sketch of one of my late "devil
fishing adventures," and I comply, yet not without
fear of disappointing your expectations. Having
already taken many, and described the capture of
several, the great charm of novelty has worn away,
and neither the capture nor the description can
be invested with their former interest. I can no
longer realize the excited feelings with which I

first surrendered myself to this manly sport—against an adversary so rarely captured, so little known, and endued, as every one believed, with a strength that made all intermeddling with him a matter of imminent peril. That strength has been mastered— and that peril so accurately measured and guarded against, that the sport, as now pursued, may be said to offer nothing more than a fair field of exercise, to such of our adventurous youth as contemplate a life of action! But, to return—I can neither recall the enthusiasm of my first feelings, nor hope to impart it; and I shall, therefore, confine myself to a simple narrative of one of my recent "days."

On the 15th of July, 1843, I set out from Bay Point on a cruise, in a good six-oared boat, manned by five oarsmen, having T. R., a cadet from West Point, and his cousin, a youth of fifteen, on board with me. E. B. M. and H. R., Esqrs., were in another boat. We stretched across, with a north-east wind, for Hilton Head, traversing that portion of the inlet which, on former occasions, I had remarked as constituting their favorite feeding, or sporting ground. We passed onward as far as Mrs. Elliott's plantation, without seeing a fish. Indeed, we were not much surprised at this, for we were anticipating, by several weeks, the customary time of seeking for them, and looked upon the expedition somewhat in the light of a reconnoisance. Our consort, discouraged by the non-appearance of the fish, and the appearance of some inopportune thunder-clouds, turned the head of his boat to the east, and moved to Bay Point; while we, preferring to prolong the cruise, landed at Mrs. Elliott's and, leaving a look-out man on the bluff, to report if the fish made their appearance, walked up to the house to partake of a collation that we had provided. At half ebb we set out on our return, and had reached the Bay Gall breaker, when, close to the bank, a devil-fish showed himself on the surface. Before I could reach the bow, and prepare my harpoon, he had disappeared; and we drifted down a quarter of a mile without seeing him again. I had scarcely resumed my place at the stern, when he appeared just under the bow of the boat; and had I not gone aft, I must certainly have struck him. Again he sunk; but I now resolved to remain at my post, and not suffer another surprise. A thunder-squall was in our rear, and the wind, veering to the east, was blowing so strong, that a short, chopping sea was raised, and I found it impossible, from the pitching of the boat, to stand on the forecastle; so I took post (standing on the bottom of the boat), as near to the bow as I could comfortably get. I did not wait long before the fish rose, and, as he crossed the bow with one of those rapid circular movements, so characteristic of this species, I made a cast at him; but from my unsteady footing, and the imperfect view of him (the tip of the wing only being visible, and the water exceedingly turbid), I missed him. Again he sunk, and when he next rose, showed his whole back above the surface. From over-anxiety, I threw the harpoon too soon, it fell short, and slightly grazed him, without entering the flesh. The fish darted off in alarm, and rose fifty yards ahead, with a demi-vault in the air! The young cadet has the helm—and as the fish shows himself, now here, now there, heads the boat in the direction —while the oarsmen, with straining sinews, sweep after him in silence. Before we can overtake him, he sinks, is invisible for five minutes together, then suddenly reappears in some unexpected direction. Not a word is spoken—the staff of the harpoon silently indicates the point—and again we press forward to assail him. And now, to our great gratification, we find that two other devil-fish had joined company; and this giving greater assurance of success, I determined to select the largest fish, and await a fairer chance for the next throw. The roughness of the water, while it disqualified the harpooner from taking steady aim, rendered the fish insensible to the noise of the oars, or the approach of the boat.

The largest fish now turned to go against the tide —this made his movements slower—and, as he brought his broad black back to the surface, I cast the harpoon, and had the satisfaction to see it this time take effect near the centre of his back-bone. Away he flew, the staff, which was firmly driven in the socket, disappearing with the harpoon, and we payed out rope to him merrily, as he swept away

for his fastnesses in the deep. When twenty-five
fathoms were out, we took a turn round the stem,
and gave him the full resistance of the boat. The
iron held bravely; but his runs, though rapid, were
short—and I soon inferred from his stopping and
hugging the bottom, that my aim had been deadly!
These runs, however intermitted, were all toward
the sea; and we found ourselves passing the last
point of Hilton Head, without any assurance that
he might not take us over the bar before flood-tide;
in which case we must cut our line and lose the fish.
It was necessary, therefore, to give him a check;
and we manned oars and rowed against him, to
draw him to the surface. The manœuvre succeeded;
and we soon had the satisfaction to see him rise to
within a few feet of the top, his proximity being
shown by the staff of the harpoon, still fixed in its
socket, and standing up perpendicularly from his
back! The thunder-cloud had now passed away,
the wind had fallen, the sea had become smooth,
and mounting the forecastle, which now afforded
secure footing, I pitched my lance with all my force
and saw it planted alongside of the harpoon, the two
staves bristling up from the back of the fish, while
a gush of blood from the new wound crimsoned the
surface of the sea. Away he dashed, and the stout
cord that held the lance snapped like a pack-thread,
leaving the iron fixed in his body, while the staff,
broken in fragments, floated to the surface. By the

same effort, the staff of the harpoon is disengaged, floats, and is taken on board.

Again the fish bears away for the sea, and we meet him by the same resistance of the oars. But he has now been taught that danger awaits him at the surface: he shuns it, and plunges downward for the bottom. It comes to a dead pull; and we have to choose between the risk of drawing out the harpoon, or being carried out to sea. We take the former, and having no efficient lance left to annoy him, determine, if the opportunity offers, to make use of the gun. After a long effort, we succeed in drawing him up; and when he once more showed himself to the light, we could observe the spearhead, with a portion of the broken staff, still sticking out from his back. The harpoon had drawn considerably from its former hold, and the wound made by it had worried into a frightful gash, more than six inches in length. Another such hard pull, and the iron may tear out. It becomes an urgent matter to dispatch him at once. His head emerges from the water, the gun, with a charge of sixteen buckshot, is levelled, the whole charge is driven into him, and a jet of blood, with his next expiration, is cast several feet into the air. The fish lay for an instant stunned—then plunged about madly, tossing himself quite over upon his back—then righting himself, and skimming over the surface with expanded wings, dashed his head blindly against the bow of the boat. Amidst these plunges and

convulsions of the dying animal, it was impossible
to keep a tight line or an equable pull; and we
exchanged looks of dismay, when we found that the
harpoon had been torn out! We drew it into the
boat, twisted and strained, but unbroken; and I
looked undeserved reproaches at this tried and true
weapon (which had already compassed the death of
four devil-fish), as if the passive instrument had
been in fault. What a disappointment!—to lose him
thus, in his very last struggle! A gleam of hope
shoots across us! In this last struggle, he *might*
rise to the surface. It is possible yet to recover him.
Let us prepare for it. In a moment the harpoon is
straightened, the staff is refitted, and scarcely is it
done, when, "There! by heavens! there he is! fifty
yards ahead, floundering on the water! Now for it,
boys!—reach him before he sinks!" Alas! he has
already sunk!

The turbid waters of the river have now given
place to the transparent green of the sea, through
which objects are distinctly visible for feet below;
and look, he is rising again from his depths! every
struggle and contortion of the agonized monster is
clearly to be seen, as he shoots upward to the light.
He is upon his back—his white feelers thrown aloft
above his head, like giant hands upraised in suppli-
cation. There was something almost *human* in the
attitude and the expression of his agony—and a
feeling quite out of keeping with the scene stole
over me while I meditated the fatal blow. It passed

away in an instant; and as he emerges from the water, the harpoon cleaves the air and is driven home into his head. A shout of exultation bursts from the crew. To have *thus* recovered him, was, indeed, a gratification. The gun is once more brought to bear—another shot, and he is still; all to the singular movements of his feelers, which, plying restlessly about his head, curl and unfold with all the flexibility of an elephant's snout. Through the tough cartilage of one of these feelers the rope is passed, and we have him safe.

And now we look about, to determine on the best mode of securing and landing our prize. We are under the Hilton Head shore, abreast of Joyner's Bank—the ebb-tide is still taking us seaward—but that best-tempered of winds, the sea-breeze, is just springing up to help us. We pass our ropes to the stern—draw the head of the fish close up to lessen the resistance—head the boat to Bay Point, and spread both our sails to the favoring breeze; and now the force of oars is added—but we make little progress in towing our fish against the current.

What has become of our consort all the while? Has the eager zeal of our young sportsmen evaporated quite? Are they asleep, that they do not spy us out and come to our assistance? True to the letter! The same sea-breeze that was filling our sails, was fanning them into slumbers undisturbed by dreams of devil-fish, or fears of friends in jeopardy. But there were watchful eyes upon us

from the shore; and when it was observed that the
boat which had steered west in the morning, was
now seen in the southeast, reduced to a mere speck
on the horizon, the whole truth was inferred. The
sleepers are awakened, and make amends for their
forgetfulness by the most strenuous efforts to come
to our assistance. Their boat is manned, and pulls
lustily toward us. And now the ebb-tide has
expended itself, and the first swell of the flood is
lending its force in aid of the wind, in taking us
toward the desired point, when we observe a speck
upon the water, which, enlarging by degrees, presents us with the wished-for boat and welcome faces
of our friends from shore. Having cheered us,
they row round to take a view of our prize—then
pass a rope round the stem of our boat, and, pulling
ahead, relieve us of a portion of our toil. In less
than five hours from the time he was struck, we
had him landed on Bay Point; and a party of
ladies, then on a visit there, were gratified in having
an opportunity of observing this singular animal,
which, from size as well as peculiarity of structure,
may well be accounted as one of the wonders of the
deep. He measured seventeen feet across the back,
and was so heavy, that the force of fifteen men was
insufficient to draw him to high water mark, though
sliders were placed beneath to assist his progress.

                                                PISCATOR.

Early in the summer of 1844, I suffered from an attack of fever, which induced me to visit Bay Point, during the month of June. When convalescent, I found excursions after devil-fish, protected from the heat by a sun-awning, a most agreeable restorative. I transfer, from my note-book, a journal of my proceedings for several days, which, though minutely detailed, I trust may not prove tedious.

JOURNAL.

BAY POINT, June 20th, 1844.

Came down this afternoon (*Thursday*), after a rough passage, having been detained at Beaufort until the tide was two-thirds spent, by a very heavy rain.

Friday, 21st.—Went across to Hilton Head to look for devil-fish. Thunder-clouds formed while crossing the river at high water; wind southwardly; had just time to land and reach the house, when it poured. At an hour's ebb, partially cleared off; on reaching the landing, saw numbers of devil-fish close into the shore. Put off, but found them shy, showing themselves but a few seconds at a time above water, then disappearing. Could not get a chance to strike, and, after half an hour's trial, put ashore to avoid another thunder-cloud, which was following exactly in the track of the former. It rained in torrents. After it ceased, returned to Bay Point without seeing any more fish, though I traversed the ground on which they were usually found. It seems to me that I have this day seen twenty different fish; but their stay at the surface is very short—shorter, I think, than when observed later in the season.

Saturday, 22d June.—Reached Hilton Head beach at high water. Two devil-fish were playing off the landing, not thirty yards from shore. Put off after them; the noise of the oars (the water being shallow) seemed to alarm them, and they disappeared. In a short time, some others made their appearance, coming down with the tide from Skull Creek. Did not succeed in calculating their visits to the surface so accurately as to get a throw of the harpoon. After seven or eight fish had passed down with the first ebb, none others appearing, concluded to anticipate them by rowing up to the flats under Pinckney Island. Did not find them there— returned to the beach in front of the avenue at Hilton Head—remained there beyond the time of tide at which they rose the day before—they did not appear. Coasted down to Pope's, and seeing nothing, returned to Bay Point at half ebb, sorely disappointed in my cruise.

Doubtless it is the state of the weather which has produced so great a change in the *run* of the fish, in so small an interval of time. It was raining on the first day—the wind was off shore; and from both wind and rain, the shrimps and small fish, which are the food of the devil-fish, would congregate near the shore, and hence their appearance in such numbers. On the night of this day, it blew violently from the west, in such a way as to sweep the shores which had been protected the day before; hence, the small fish were driven off, and the devil-fish were not there, *because their food was not there. To find subsistence easily and abundantly, is an impulse that pervades all animal life.* It is the great law which governs the inferior animals, as well as man. Hunters and fishermen must not lose sight of this rule, but seek their game by seeking their feeding-places.

Some years back, the devil-fish were sought for only in August. Last year, for the first time, in July, and now, it appears, they may be taken in June. I am now convinced, from what I have myself observed, that they visit our inlets not occasionally only, and in limited numbers, but annually and in considerable shoals; and it indicates a very extraordinary want of observation or enterprise in our predecessors, that they have not noticed these fish, and converted them into objects of sport or profit. There is danger enough in the pastime to give it the highest relish (it is, in fact, whale-fishing in miniature); nor is it objectionable on the score of cruelty: it is not killing in mere wantonness, for the liver yields an oil useful for many agricultural purposes, and the body cut into portions convenient for transportation, and carted out upon the fields, proves an excellent fertilizer of the soil.

Sunday, 23d June.—Weather moderate and winds easterly.

Monday, 24th June.—Wind very fresh at north-east. Mr. W. Cuthbert came on board, and we sailed for Hilton Head, and reached the avenue an hour before high water. Saw a devil-fish at the landing and gave chase, but to no purpose—he was apparently feeding, and would show his wings only at long intervals, and for a few seconds at a time; so that before the boat could reach the spot he was gone. He sometimes came very close to the beach (I should say in five feet water), but would sheer off at the approach of the boat. After a fruitless pursuit of an hour, we gave him up, and cruised up to the mouth of Skull Creek. Saw nothing— returned to the landing, and visited the cotton-field. It was now four o'clock, P. M., and full quarter ebb. In a last hope to see them, loitered a while on the beach, when, just as we were making ready to get on board, a shoal of devil-fish came sweeping along the beach, travelling rapidly downward with the tide, and showing themselves more freely than any I had seen this year. I pushed at one that showed his back fairly above water, as he swam; but he sank just before I reached him, and I drove down the harpoon at a venture. He had a narrow escape, for the staff struck him. At this moment, three showed themselves below and one above. I pushed for the latter, and when I approached the spot, I saw the water boiling up like a caldron—from which sign I knew that the fish was throwing his somersets below the surface (in the way which is so very peculiar to them). Making the oarsmen check the headway with their oars, I looked anxiously for a view, when, unexpectedly, I saw the white of his belly far beneath the water, and quite away toward the stern. He was thus behind me, but wheeling suddenly to the right, I pitched the harpoon at him, across the oars, and felt a sensation of surprise, as well as pleasure, in finding that I had struck him. The fish dashed out violently for the channel, and we payed him out thirty fathoms of rope, until, headway being given to the boat, we brought him to a dead pull: and now his motions were very erratic; unlike some that I had before struck, he did not take a direct course for the sea, but sometimes drew the boat against the tide—then suddenly turned and ran directly toward us, so as to give slack line. I inferred from these signs, that he was mortally hurt. As often as he approached the Middle Bank and shoaled the water, he drew off in alarm, and would not cross it until he had got to its tail; his course was then for Paris Bank, which suiting well with our intention to land him, if we could, at Bay Point, we did not interrupt. About this time he came to the surface without being pulled, and showed great distress—and we resolved, then, to draw upon him and get a second harpoon planted. It was after various fruitless efforts, and by shortening the rope as far as we prudently could, that we at length drew him so far up, that the dark shadow of his body was indistinctly seen beneath. The second harpoon was now driven, and the gush of blood to the surface, showed that it had done its work. We now drew mainly on this second, leaving only a moderate strain upon the first—and after a few convulsive runs, brought him up helplessly to the surface, and with a spear dispatched him outright. With a hatchet we now cut a hole in one of his feelers, and inserting a rope, passed it to the stern, drawing solely on this, so that the resistance of the fish through the water should be as small as practicable. The wind was now due east, and moderately fresh; we raised both sails, and, helped at the same time by the oars, made some way in our tedious progress of towing our prize to land. At this time, espied a boat beating down from Beaufort, and on signalizing her, she proved to be that of Col. De Treville, then on his way to Bay Point. His offer of assistance was accepted, and a tow line being passed to his boat, we landed our fish at the Point exactly at sunset. This fish measured sixteen feet across, which I suppose to be the medium size of those that visit our waters. The first harpoon had struck it near the centre of the belly—had pierced the liver, and passed nearly through to the back. The second had passed from the back into his lungs or gills—so that the full power of so large a fish was never fairly exerted against us. Had the same fish been struck in the wings, or other parts not vital, his capture would have been uncertain, and would at any rate have cost us the work of many hours.

I suppose the shoal of devil-fish was a large one; the third which appeared we struck at—the fourth we harpooned—and as we were rapidly drawing off from the shore, a fifth was seen. How many were still behind, we had no leisure to observe; but conjecture this was but the advance guard of the column.

I made no further notes of my excursions at the time, but will add that prior to my departure for the North, in July of this year, I had struck seven of these fish, and captured four.

In 1845, these sports were renewed; but under aspects that offer but little novelty to the reader. The devil-fish were reported to be in force in Broad River, during the month of June; but no expeditions were planned against them during that month. Early in July, E. B. M., already known to the reader of these "Sports," made a cruise after them, and, on the second day's search, succeeded in capturing one. On Wednesday, the 16th, I made my first venture— saw five and captured one. On the next day, being joined by Mr. M., we sallied out in our respective boats, and found them in force. I think we could not have seen fewer than fifteen. But the weather was unpropitious, and though we struck five, and probably killed the greater part of them, we could

not affirm with certainty that we had captured one.
Once, during the day, I enjoyed a solitary run, and
twice a run in company—both boats being engaged
at the same time, and the fish running in the same
parallel. Two hours before nightfall, each boat
then having a fish in tow, we were overtaken by a
perfect tempest. A black and fearful looking
thunder-cloud lay brooding over the bay, and
seemed to descend to the very waters, and be com-
mingled with them. It was extreme rashness, in
our undecked boats, to brave the anger of the storm;
and, by a simultaneous movement, we resolved to
force up our fish, so as either to lose or capture
them before it should burst upon us. The harpoon
of my consort tore out when the fish was drawn
to the surface, and almost "in articulo mortis." In
my own case, the fish, struck through the branchial
processes, and evidently at his last gasp, snapt
asunder the harpoon and escaped, leaving the barb
in his body. Thus released from our fish (for in all
my service, I have never severed a rope or volun-
tarily disengaged myself from a devil-fish), we
lifted a hand's breadth of canvas to the gust which
was now upon us, and made our escape to the shore.
We had capital and very exciting sport; but considered our victory somewhat incomplete, because
we had not carried off the bodies of the slain.

The next day, strengthened by an accession of
new adventurers, we tried our luck again; but
the fish were gone—all their sporting grounds were

visited, but in vain; and we came reluctantly to the
conclusion, that these were not of that description
of game which increased the faster for being
destroyed—a paradox seriously maintained by more
than one sportsman who could be named.

After a week's pause, we tried them again; but
very few were seen, and they uncommonly shy.
One was taken from Mr. Heyward's boat, being
harpooned by Mr. Cuthbert; and, on the day following, another, seemingly the sole survivor of the
field, was captured by myself. This closes, thus
far, the adventures of the season. Whether they
have been alarmed by the touch of the harpoon,
or the loss of their companions, and are prompted
by their instinct to avoid the grounds on which
they have suffered persecution—or whether, during
the prevailing unexampled drought, they have
ascended the rivers in search of subsistence—are
questions which we have no data satisfactorily to
answer.

The chase of the devil-fish may now be said to
be an established diversion of the planters in the
vicinity of Port Royal Sound. They make Bay
Point their place of rendezvous, and, well-provided
with lances and harpoons, sally forth in search of
them, at or about high water—when they enter the
inlet to feed upon the shrimps, and small fish that
abound along the shores. On the ebb tide they

retire again to sea—so that the time for seeking
them is confined to a few hours in the day. They
feed mostly upon the windward shores of the inlet,
where the small fish chiefly congregate; and their
presence upon the feeding ground is indicated by
a slight projection above the water of one of their
wings. The motion is so rapid and bird-like, that
none who have once seen it will mistake, or ascribe
it to any other fish. Sometimes, though not often,
you may approach him while feeding in shallow
water, near enough to strike; but the best opportunity is offered by waiting quietly near the spot
where he has disappeared, until, having ceased to
feed, he strikes out for the deep water, and having
reached it, begins a series of somersets that give
the sportsman an excellent chance to strike him.
It is a very curious exhibition. You first see the
feelers thrown out of the water; then the white
stomach, marked with five gills, or branchial apertures, on each side (for the fish is on his back)—
then his tail emerges. After a disappearance for a
few seconds, the revolution is repeated—sometimes
as often as six times. It happens, occasionally that
in making these somersets, the fish does not rise
quite to the surface, but is several feet below; so
that his revolutions are detected by the appearance
and disappearance of the white or under part of
his body, dimly seen through the turbid water in
which he delights. Sometimes, indeed, he is unseen;
but his presence is shown to the observant sports-

man by the boiling of the water from below, as from a great caldron. With no better guide than this, the harpoon has been darted down, and reached him when twelve feet below the surface.

What purpose the fish effects by these strange motions, I leave to naturalists to determine. Perhaps, while in this supine posture, he rejects the water from his complicated strainers and retains the small fish to be swallowed, for I have remarked the gills alternately expanded and collapsed, while he executed the manœuvre. But this is mere conjecture, and I may come nearer to the mark in another suggestion, which I intend to offer in a subsequent chapter.

When one of these fish is struck, he commonly darts off with great rapidity, running out the forty fathoms of rope, and then dragging along the boat with quite as much speed as is agreeable. If several boats are in company, they usually attach themselves to the first, and the little fleet is dragged merrily along.

The prudent sportsman will not draw too violently on him at first, but will suffer him to exhaust himself by his efforts; when he is as quietly as possible drawn to the surface, by putting three or four hands to the rope. When seen, a second harpoon is driven into his body. Then commences the serious conflict. He is forced up by the line—he flounders and lashes the waves with his immense wings, or plunges desperately for the bottom, to

which he sometimes *clings for hours*, till, exhausted
at last, he yields to the force which draws him to
the surface, and is dispatched with many wounds.

Occasionally, after having three harpoons fastened in him, and as many lances plunged into his
body, he strikes out indomitably for the ocean, and
escapes—leaving the sportsmen to make their way
as best they may, to the distant land. I have been
carried twenty-five miles, in the course of a few
hours by two of these fish (having struck a relay
when my first sea-horse escaped, and losing both),
with three boats in train!

The reader must not suppose that there is no risk
in the pursuit and capture of such formidable game.
The spice of danger mingling with this sport,
serves to increase its relish. He who wields the
harpoon, should have a quick eye, a steady arm,
and a cool head; for if he loses his presence of
mind, and suffers himself to be entangled in the
rope, during the first furious runs of the fish, he
may lose his life. But no precautions can absolutely secure the sportsman against danger; a truth
which had nearly been brought home to me in a
manner peculiarly painful—as the incident I am
about to relate will serve to illustrate.

I had left the cruising ground but a few days,
when a party was formed, in July, 1844, to engage
in this sport. Nath. Heyward, Jun., J. G. Barnwell, E. B. Means, and my son, Thos. R. S. Elliott,
were respectively in command of a boat each, accom-

panied by several of their friends. While these
boats were lying on their oars, expecting the
approach of fish, one showed himself far ahead,
and they all started in pursuit. It was my son's
fortune to reach him first. His harpoon had scarcely
pierced him, when the fish made a demi-vault in
the air, and, in his descent, struck the boat violently
with one of his wings. Had he fallen perpendicularly on the boat, it must have been crushed, to the
imminent peril of all on board. As it happened, the
blow fell aslant upon the bow—and the effect was
to drive her astern with such force, that James Cuthbert, Esq., of Pocotaligo, who was at the helm, was
pitched forward at full length on the platform.
Each oarsman was thrown forward beyond the seat
he occupied; and my son, who was standing on the
forecastle, was projected far beyond the bow of the
boat. He fell, not into the sea, but directly upon
the back of the devil-fish, who lay in full sprawl
on the surface. For some seconds Tom lay out of
the water, on the back of this veritable Kraken,
but happily made his escape without being entangled
in the cordage, or receiving a parting salute from
his formidable wings. He was an expert swimmer,
and struck off for the boat. The fish, meantime,
had darted beneath, and was drawing her astern.
My henchman, Dick, who was the first to recover his
wits, tossed overboard a coil of rope, and extended
an oar, the blade of which was seized by my son,
who thus secured his retreat to the boat. He had

no sooner gained footing in it, than, standing on
the forecastle, he gave three hearty cheers, and
thus assured his companions of his safety. They,
meantime, from their several boats, had seen his
perilous situation, without the chance of assisting
him; their oarsmen, when ordered to pull ahead,
stood amazed or stupefied, and dropping their oars
and jaws, cried out, "Great King! Mass Tom overboard!" So intense was their curiosity to see how
the affair would end, that they entirely forgot how
much might depend on their own efforts. Could
they have rowed and looked at the same time, it
would have been all very well; but to turn their
backs on such a pageant, every incident of which
they were so keenly bent on observing, was expecting
too much from African forethought and self-
possession!

In a few minutes my son found himself surrounded by his companions, whose boats were closely
grouped around. They threw themselves into action
with a vivacity which showed that they were disposed to punish the fish for the insolence of his
attack. They allowed him but short time for shrift,
and forcing him to the surface, filled his body with
their resentful weapons; then, joining their forces,
drew him rapidly to the shore, and landed him,
amidst shouts and cheerings, at Mrs. Elliott's,
Hilton Head. He measured sixteen feet across!

The love of human flesh, ascribed by Oppian to a
fish (conjectured to be the devil-fish) which was

said to destroy the mariner, by sinking him to the
bottom and smothering him beneath his enormous
wings, must be considered as fabulous; for the fish,
in this case, was as ready to fly from the mariner,
as the mariner from him—unless it be said (as, in
truth, it might be) that, being transfixed by a
harpoon, the fish was just then not in condition to
indulge his propensity. But, apart from this, his
whole structure forbids the supposition of his
making *man* his *prey!* The other characteristic of
Oppian is just. He is "Eurotatos pantessin met
ichthusin"—*the broadest among fish.*

A singular incident occurred as they were towing
their prize against the current towards the shore.
A devil-fish appeared above, directly in their course,
and bearing down swiftly for them. One of our
sportsmen (knowing his modesty, I purposely withhold his name, "since he might blush to find it
fame;" whom, nevertheless, we will call—since he
must have a name—simply, "*John*"), uncoiling his
legs, which had been stowed away under him in
the stern-seat, now started up in excitement, and
striding over the heads of his crew, planted himself
in the forecastle; then stretched his long right arm
aloft, and hurled his harpoon into the advancing
monster with the force of a catapult. To cut loose
from the convoy, and dash away on his own hook,
was the work of a moment; and the manœuvre was
happily executed, without loss of limb or other
material accident or entanglement. This was a

pleasant episode in the main action; but the rule
which I have prescribed for myself in these narratives, will not allow me to say that our sportsmen
added *this* to the number of their trophies, for the
fish escaped after a run of several miles; through
no want of force in the hand that wielded the harpoon certainly, for John has brought down from
his ancestors a strong right arm, that would have
done no discredit to county Galway.

This strength was not unattended by generosity,
for, on one occasion, when John was cruising for
devil-fish, he forgot "to give point," and came down
"whack" on the head of his adversary with the flat
of his harpoon, and with such amazing emphasis,
that the diabolic was completely stunned and
thrown off "his fence." Instead of diving, as a
discreet fish was bound to do, he rose to the surface, lolling out his great eyes at John, as much as
to ask, "what the deuce he meant, by dealing him
such a confounded blow?" For some minutes, the
fish kept skimming about the boat—his wide flaps
fluttering, bird-like, over the surface—while John
in turn, opened his eyes in astonishment at the
singular exhibition. Whether he thought that his
adversary came to ask an explanation, and "be
resolved whether that ———— ———— so unkindly
knocked or no," or whether he looked upon it as
a sort of compliment, paid after the aquatic fashion
of his Galwegian force, I don't pretend to say; but
certain it is, that while he had him *down, as it*

were, and off his guard, John *did not repeat the blow!* In a few minutes, the fish, flourishing his tail aloft by way of salute, plunged downwards for his depths, and doubtless reported to his compatriots the hard usage he had received from a denizen of the thinner element above. In another minute the sea closed over him—his wake was no more seen— not a ripple was left on the surface, and the incidents just told, living only in the memory of the sportsman, seemed vague and shadowy as a dream.

———

Subsequently to the publication of the first edition of "Carolina Sports," I made frequent expeditions in pursuit of devil-fish; but I shall not tax the patience of my reader by more than an occasional allusion to them. So similar in general were the incidents attending them, that the narrative of one, might almost serve for all. Instead of detailed statements of these excursions, therefore, the reader may expect to find in the pages now appended, only such incidents as are new, or such suggestions as may serve to throw light on what is obscure or unexplained in the habits of the fish.

What is here said may at least afford matter of speculation to the students of natural history, should any such honor these pages with a perusal.

But it will be interesting to the sportsman, as well as to the naturalist, to know what is the ordinary food of the devil-fish. I have frequently examined the contents of their stomachs, and found little else in them than portions of shell-fish, highly triturated, resembling the shells of shrimps. Once a small crab was found entire; but I sought in vain for the scales of small fish, which I supposed to be their food, partly because the devil-fish make their appearance in our waters in *May*, before the shrimps are found on our shores, and would thus be anticipating their food—a mistake which fish are not apt to make—and partly because I witnessed a performance on the part of a devil-fish, which could scarcely be referred to anything else but to an occasional indulgence in a fish diet.

I was watching a devil-fish, who was playing close to the shore. But in shallow water he is often alarmed by the noise of the oars, and he would not suffer my approach within striking distance. While thus engaged, I observed a shoal of small mullets swimming near the surface, and showing signs of extraordinary agitation, when suddenly the open mouth of the devil-fish was protruded from below, and the small fry disappeared from view, and were received into it, as into the mouth of an enormous funnel. I do not think it was mere wantonness on the part of the fish, but that he was, on that occasion, indulging a caprice of appetite, and substituting a diet of scale-fish for his ordinary mess of shrimps.

On the first of July, 1846, I launched my boat at

Bay Point, and crossed over to the Hilton Head shore in search of devil-fish. I was accompanied by Henry M. Stuart, Esq.

It was high water about four o'clock p. m., and on reaching the landing at Mrs. Elliott's, just as the tide was turning, we saw three or more. They did not show themselves *somersetting* for some time, but after a while, began to sport, and throw somersets under the water, but so near to the surface as to show their bellies in the evolution. We saw, I do not doubt, as many as twenty fish. We counted eleven that leaped entirely out of the water. They were in the channel, and were further from shore than where we had usually met with them; and, on approaching near to them in our boat, we remarked that those which leaped entirely out of the water, did not again show themselves on the surface, until they had silently gone a mile or so toward the sea, when they reappeared, gambolled awhile, threw new somersets, and again disappeared for a new seaward movement. The fish which were behind, came along sporting, until they had reached the spot where the first had thrown their somersets. They, too, then threw their somersets, and disappeared like the first. Usually they leaped twice— leaping from their backs, and falling likewise on their backs; leaping, I should say, at least ten feet above the water.

After some delay (for early in the season they do not stand the point), I struck a fish, which resisted

very moderately for a good half hour, when it
made some furious runs, giving me to think that the
sharks had gotten the scent of his blood, and were
in fierce pursuit. The winds had been hard from
the south for several days, and the weather was
now so squally and threatening, that I became
anxious to complete the capture of the fish before
night; so I planted a second harpoon, and then, as
occasion offered, gave him the spear. When drawn
up alongside, he began to make short, circular runs,
and twisted the two ropes together, so that they
could not be separated. The thunder muttered, and
the dark cloud still approached us from the southwest, spreading its wings beyond us on every side,
so as to leave no chance of escape; so we had to force
on the lines, and draw the fish close up to the boat.
When the lurching from the high sea snapped off,
first one, and then the other of the stout ropes,
leaving both harpoons fixed in the fish, which was
thus uselessly killed. Soon as we were released, we
pushed for the shore at Bay Point, which we
scarcely reached before the storm was down upon us.

Thursday, 2d July.—Set out on another cruise
today. The weather threatening; wind blowing
fresh from the south. H. M. S. and E. M. prom-
ising to man a boat and come to my assistance, if
they observed me succeed in harpooning a fish.
Saw but few leap today; did not find them so
numerous under the Hilton Head shore. Struck at
one while somersetting below the surface; the

harpoon bounded off without entering; probably it encountered the fore part of the head, in which point they are invulnerable. Soon after, found myself in a group where four were sporting. Pushed at one on the right; he disappeared, when a very large fish unexpectedly rose to my left, and showed himself so fairly that I unadvisedly pitched the harpoon into him. The first draw of the rope— *was across my neck!* Not so pleasant that. Spinning myself out of the coil, I leaped clear of it, and he ran out the whole line before we checked him with the weight of the boat. Like the fish struck the day before, he made some violent runs, and left us this time no doubt as to the cause; for, when drawn up, he thrust out one of his fins, still bleeding, from which the tip had been just cut by a shark; his enemy, in all likelihood, being yet in pursuit. I plunged the spear so deeply into his body that it passed through him, and the cord attached to it was drawn through my hand as he ran and carried it off along with the spear. When next drawn up, I gave him a desperate wound on the back with my remaining spear. He was now much exhausted, and we brought him up to the stern with a short rope, and attempted to draw him to the land. The wind was very high from south and the fish had taken us down the centre channel, abreast of Joyner's Bank, and, by setting the foresail, and bearing him down toward the Bay Point shore, I was getting the leeway for my reckoning, when the rising of the squall obliged me again to look for safety. The clouds seemed highly charged with electricity, and came sweeping onward with fearful rapidity. While there was any chance of killing the fish in time for reaching the shore in advance of the storm, I held on to my play, which would eventually have succeeded, but night and the tempest were both upon me, and I drew him closer to the stern, that I might kill him at once, or, if that were impracticable, might, at least, disengage my harpoon. At this moment, the rope parted. But what was my surprise at beholding the fish, though now released, still keeping company with us, swimming close to the boat and following us with his horns projected on each side of the stern, moving exactly with our speed, and in our direction! I caught at my spear; but one glance at the lowering sky served to show the futility of making further onslaught on him. To reach the shore before the storm should burst on us, was the imperious demand now made on us by controlling circumstances, and we spread our main-sail, and flew away from the gale and from the devil-fish, not without casting some anxious looks behind, to see if he still pursued. But our speed was too great; he fell behind, and we saw him no more!

Shall I say that no touch of superstitious feeling took momentary possession of my mind, in witnessing an act so startling, on a scene so wild? What if he pursued us, impelled by the instinct of vengeance? What if he leaped upon us in that vindictive mood? In that retributory leap, our boat would be crushed like a cockle-shell. Shall I say, that fancies such as these did not flit across our minds, while the night deepened, and the lightnings flashed around us, and the whitening waves were dashed aside from our prow, as we sped over the waste of waters?

But in sober earnest, what could have been the purpose of the fish in following us after his release? Can the naturalist tell? Perhaps the sharks were still pursuing him, and he found the presence of the boat a protection; or perhaps he followed the boat because the slime from his own body, having been rubbed off against its sides, he was misled by the pungency of the smell into the belief that he was following one of his own tribe, whose companionship he sought in the extremity of his misery. Some motive there must have been for a proceeding so strange.

To solve the problem by a reference to the sense of smell, will not appear unreasonable to those who have remarked how accurately these fish follow each other, though miles apart, and in cases wherein, from the turbid state of the water, *sight* could have been of no avail for their direction. May not this high leaping from the water, and consequent fall, be designed to diffuse this slime and the scent that belongs to it, so as to assure the rest of the tribe of the course taken by their predecessors? Is it not

6—C. S.

in truth the means provided by nature by which they signal each other, and contrive to pursue the same tiack through the expanse of ocean? May not, in short, their gambollings on the surface, and their somersets beneath, have the self-same purpose, and be explained by this hypothesis?

The squall struck us before we gained the shore, and the rain fell upon us with a stunning and bewildering effect; but all was unheeded in the satisfaction of finding ourselves once more on firm land, safe from the tempest and the startling and unwelcome pursuit to which we have just referred!

The storms of these two successive evenings which had twice prevented me from landing my fish, were extensive and exceedingly violent, destroying fences, uprooting trees, and falling on some devoted spots with the force of a tornado. Fortunately for me, though within their range, I was not in their vortex. Had it been otherwise, these narratives had not been written!

Besides the risks from storms, there is undoubtedly some risk in the encounter with these devil-fish. Whoever contends with superior force must do so at some peril; but by prudence and forecast these dangers can be greatly abated, and I remember but one occasion on which I found myself decidedly imperilled by the fish itself. A fish had been struck and drawn repeatedly to the boat's side, but we could not hold him there; he floundered and plunged so violently that we were forced to give him line, which he drew out until he reached the bottom; leaving us the toil of drawing him again to the surface. We had on board a large iron hook and tiller made expressly for such service (the hook, however, being without a barb), and on his next appearance I plunged it into the fish, and passed it over to one of the boatmen, directing him to hold on. Then arming myself with a large knife (for he still struggled vigorously), I passed my arm over the gunwale of the boat, and began to strike him with this new weapon, as he lay a foot or so beneath the water. Suddenly, my hand was paralyzed, and the reader will understand my feelings when looking into the water, I found that the devil-fish had seized my arm with one of his feelers, and pressed it powerless against his body! "He stays my arm—pleads for mercy—appeals like an intelligent creature to my humanity," was my first thought. "He has bound me to his fate," was the startling conviction that dispelled that first thought, and revealed to me the imminent peril in which I stood. A fate worse than Mazeppa's will be mine if he breaks loose again! "For God's sake, boys, hold on! He has clutched my arm, and if he runs again for bottom, my life goes with him!" How long then seemed to me those few brief moments of uncertainty; but they are past, his force is exhausted, his hold on me relaxes, and in his very death struggle, my arm again is free! I took my seat with sobered feelings, thinking by how narrow

a chance the pursuer had escaped the fate of his
victim!

On another occasion there occurred something
worth relating, which, that I might not offend the
delicacy of the fastidious, I have turned into Latin,
trusting that, thus forewarned, they will not go out
of their way to read it.

I had observed a fish in Skull Creek channel
taking his course toward the sea. Shortly after, I
saw another, taking precisely the same track. The
first then turned toward the Hilton Head shore,
so did the second. I silently pursued them, until
they approached within one hundred yards of the
beach, in the hope of striking one or the other of
them. Then checking the speed of the boat, while
the boatmen lay on their oars, prepared to turn the
boat in any direction that might be required, and
while in eager expectation, I stood prepared to dart
my harpoon——

Subito, læva—sed longiore spatio, quam, si jacu-
latus essem, speraverim transfigere ictu—duos
pisces cephalopteras aspexi, amplexu conjunctos.
Ventribus juxtapositis—capitibus erectis, et supra
undam oblatis—antennis lascive intersertis—coitum
salacem, ut solet genus squalus, ipso contactu
corporis, tunc sine dubio exercuere. Ferire, ob
distantiam non licitum, aut duos cephelopteras,
solo ictu transfixisse, gloria inopinata mihi con-
tegisset. Cymbam appropinquantem, hastamque
minantem, circumspecte evitant—et, in profundo

paulisper latentes, iterum, dextra emergunt, ludosque lascivos repetunt. Tunc, quasi deliciis satiati, saltatione in aëre, utrinque facta—apertum mare petivere. Hoc concursu tam raro notato—antennis albis, cum nigris admixis utsi lacertis—imago fœdi et immundi coitus, nudi Africani cum Caucasiana, plane præfigurabatur.

The devil-fish, as they frequent indifferently the deep and shallow portions of the coast, do not seem in their normal state to dread the attack of the sharks. They probably defend themselves by the blows of their formidable wings, or protect themselves by their superior swiftness from the terrible jaws of that sea-scourge. But the case is different when the devil-fish has been harpooned; the sharks, attracted by the scent of his blood, then surround him, while striving to disengage himself from the fatal harpoon, and taking him at disadvantage, attempt to destroy him. This we know, from the desperate and unexpected runs made by the devil-fish—by the bleeding fin, which as I have elsewhere described, the fish exhibited when drawn to the surface—and conclusively, by the actual assault of the shark, on the surface, as once witnessed by myself. We had one day struck a fish, which, resisting longer than usual, had carried us down the harbor some five or six miles outside of land. When we had mastered him, we set sail and attempted to tow him to land. While thus engaged, the fish, drawn close up under the stern, turned over upon his back by the action of the boat, and thus exposed to view his white belly, at the depth of four or five feet below the surface. I was steering, but casting my eyes back to observe whether the fish was so secured as to offer the minimum of resistance in our towing process, I was startled to perceive that a large shark was lying over the fish; his size and position being well defined, by the contrast of color. I called for another harpoon, but none other was rigged at the moment; so striking at him with a spear, he made his retreat; and when we landed the devil-fish, I was surprised to find that, short as the time apparently was, during which he had occupied the position in which I saw him, he had contrived, nevertheless, to cut out from the soft and yielding belly of the fish, a piece as large as could be compassed by his outspread jaws.

What I might have done, in the case just related, had the harpoon been ready for the attempt, has actually been done by Mr. Ed. B. Means, already mentioned in the earlier pages of this book. He was cruising in his sailboat, along the Hilton-Head shore, while it was yet flood tide, and seeing a fish (though they do not usually show themselves until ebb tide), succeeded in striking it. The fish ran with the tide, which soon brought him up with the north point of Pinckney Island. He had plunged his spear into the fish so as to cause him to bleed freely, when he was attacked by a large shovel-nosed or hammer-headed shark.

In his effort to escape from this new enemy, the devil-fish made a rapid turn, which passed the harpooner's rope round the neck of the shark, making a very effective noose, from which, by reason of his hammer-head, he could not escape—the greater the fright of the devil-fish—the faster he fled—the harder he drew the noose around the neck of his assailant, so that Mr. Means had time to fling a new harpoon into the intrusive shark, and enjoyed the singular satisfaction of landing a devil-fish and a shark by the same line! This landing was effected on a bank lying to the northwest of Pinckney Island; and our sportsman towed the shark over to Bay Point, and landed it on the beach. I saw it after it was landed. It was a formidable-looking creature, measuring twelve feet in length!

Having ascertained the fact that the sharks attack the devil-fish when wounded, we frequently prepare ourselves with chain-hooks, and lines, and throwing our baits overboard, troll for sharks, while we are being drawn about by devil-fish! That fish is thus made to act as a decoy for the sharks, and I have known five sharks taken before the devil-fish was mastered.

The porpoises do not appear to attack the devil-fish (though I have known them to attack a grampus whale, and drive him ashore). They seem, however, to avoid each other, and it is a common

remark among our sportsmen, that when the shoals
of porpoises are frequent in our waters, the devil-
fish are scarce!

———

Since, among the readers of this book of "Sports,"
there may be some who would desire to peruse a
scientific description of the devil-fish, I have sub-
joined one, taken from the latest authority, viz.,
from the "Zoology of New York. By James E.
De Kay. Albany: 1842."

"Family Raiidæ.

"Genus Cephaloptera. Dumeril.

"The pectorals produced into long processes at
their anterior extremities, presenting the appearance of two horns. Teeth slender; dorsal small;
tail slender, with a serrated spine.

"The Sea-Devil.

"Cephalopetera Vampirus.

"The Vampire of the Ocean.—Mitchell. Cephalopetera giorna.—Lesueur.

"Characteristics.—Tail longer than the body, and
armed with one or more spines; dorsal between the
ventrals; anterior margin of the pectorals convex;
posterior concave; width, 16-18 feet.

"Description.—Body large; the transverse much
exceeding its longitudinal diameter. Skin rough to
the touch, as in many species of Squalus, but without
any evident tubercles or spines. Head not distinct
from the body, subtruncate in front, slightly convex.

Mouth subterminal, with very small teeth, in seven or eight rows, in the lower jaw distant and in quincunx; those of the upper jaw scarcely visible. Nostrils small, and placed near the angles of the mouth, two feet apart. Eyes prominent, lateral, four feet apart, and placed on an eminence at the base of the frontal appendices. Branchial apertures narrow, linear, varying from one to two feet in length, with valvular coverings. Tail long, slender, sub-compressed, terminating in a slender extremity.

"The dorsal fin small, triangular, with thirty-six rays, and placed over the base of the tail between the ventrals; a short, serrated spine, just anterior to it. Pectorals much elongated, pointed, arched in front, concave behind, the frontal appendices projected on each side of the mouth, and used as instruments of prehension; they are two feet and a half long, and a foot wide. Ventrals broad, short, deeply emarginated and rounded behind, continuous in front with the pectorals.

"Color.—Blue-black above; dusky, varied with large opaque white clouds, beneath.

"Length to the base of the tail, 10 feet; to the end of the tail, 16 feet; width across the tips of the pectorals, 17 feet.

"This is one of those large monsters of the deep, which are occasionally captured along our shores. It was first noticed by Catesby, on the coast of Carolina, where it appears to be more frequent than further north. The next notice is by Dr. Mitchell, cited above, from a specimen captured at the mouth of Delaware Bay. Another individual was taken in Savannah, in 1824. Lesueur, who described it anew from the specimen examined by Dr. Mitchell, considered it as identical with the R. giorna of Lacépède. I have carefully compared these descriptions, and find too many striking dissimilarities to enable me to consider them as identical. In this view I am sustained by Cuvier, in the last edition of the Règne Animal. The giorna rarely exceeds fifty pounds in weight, according to Risso; while our species is so large, that, according to Mitchell, it required three pair of oxen, aided by a horse and twenty-two men, to drag it to the dry land. It was estimated to weigh between four and five tons. It approaches, in fact, nearer to the C. Massena, of Risso.

"The Sea-devil, or Oceanic Vampire, as it has been not inaptly named, is known to seize the cables of small vessels at anchor, and draw them for several miles with great velocity. An instance of this kind was related to me, by a credible eyewitness, as having occurred in the harbor of Charleston. A schooner, lying at anchor, was suddenly seen moving across the harbor with great rapidity, impelled by some unknown and mysterious power. Upon approaching the opposite shore, its course was changed so suddenly, as nearly to capsize the vessel, when it again crossed the harbor with its former velocity, and the same scene was repeated when it approached the shore. These mysterious flights across the harbor were repeated several times, in the presence of hundreds of spectators, and suddenly ceased."

This description, taken from De Kay, and published but three years since, shows how very imperfect is the knowledge of the naturalists, even of the present day, in regard to this fish. The very first *characteristic*, viz: "Tail longer than the body, and armed with one or more spines," is incorrect in both particulars. In the first specification, viz., that the tail is longer than the body, the description is at variance not only with fact, but with itself; for we read further on, that the "length to the base of the tail, is ten feet; to the end of the tail sixteen"; so that the length of the tail is, to that of the body, as six to ten. This corresponds with what I have myself observed; and in all the specimens which I have examined (and they amount to almost twenty), there was not one which was armed with a spine, serrated or otherwise. The socket, or groove, where such a formidable weapon may have been placed, was found, it is true, in all; but the spine in none. It was placed below the caudal fin, and just where the spine is usually found in the sting-ray; but I do not believe that it is ever found in this fish—in which opinion I am confirmed by remarking, that the young *devil-fish-calf*, to be seen at Venuchi's exhibition-room, King Street, Charleston, is without a spine.

The story of their using their feelers as instruments of prehension, and drawing vessels about the harbor, is very like that given by Catesby (vol. i., page 32); the only difference is, that in one case it was a sloop, in the other a schooner. They were probably both true. The same thing happened about fifteen years ago, in one of the inlets on the coast of Georgia. A trading vessel lay at anchor, and, while her crew were on shore, one of these fish seized the cable and dragged her off, anchor and all, to the consternation of the sailors, who pursued their retreating bark for some miles in their boat, and regained her, when the devil-fish had contrived, or seen fit, to disengage himself from his prize.

I have often listened, when a boy, to the story of an old family servant, quite a respectable negro, whose testimony I have no reason to discredit, and which would seem to corroborate the instances already cited. He was fishing near the Hilton Head beach, for sharks; and, accompanied by another hand, was anchored about fifty·yards from shore, in a four-oared boat, when a devil-fish seized hold of the shark line. Whether he grasped the line between his feelers, or accidentally struck the hook into his body, cannot accurately be known; but he darted off with the line, dragging the boat from her anchorage, and moved seaward with such fearful velocity, that the fishermen threw themselves flat on their faces, and gave themselves up for lost. "After lying a long time in this posture," said the old man, "in expectation of death, I gained a little heart, and stealing a look over the gunwale, *saw iron swim*—there was the anchor playing duck and drake on the top of the water, while the boat was going stern-foremost for the sea! At last," said he, "we cut loose when he had almost got us out to sea." The earnestness of the old man, and the look of undissembled terror which he wore in telling the story, convince me that he spoke the truth.

I have but one observation more to make on the description of De Kay. "Color—Blue-black above; *dusky, varied with large white opaque clouds, beneath*." It would be more correct to say, "*white*, varied with large *dusky opaque clouds beneath*," for, in every case, the white has predominated, and in a few cases there were no dusky spots at all!

It will be seen, from the foregoing description, that, unlike the porpoise or the whale, the devil-fish is not obliged to come to the surface for breath. In one hour and forty minutes, the whale is obliged to show himself at the top of the water; not so the devil-fish, which the sportsman is consequently obliged to draw up by sheer force—a circumstance which greatly increases the risk of losing him.

In conclusion, I would recommend to the sportsman who goes in search of devil-fish, to embark in a four-oared boat, if sport be his object; for he will then feel the full force of the fish, and enjoy the velocity of the movement. But, if success in capturing be uppermost in his thoughts, a six-oared boat is to be preferred. In either case, it should be without a keel, and draw but little water forward; for a rapid change of front is necessary, as well in the attack as the pursuit.

I well know the disposition that prevails to treat such sporting incidents as are unusual, or which *we* happen not to have witnessed, as exaggerations involving a material departure from truth. Willing as I may be to amuse others with these narratives, I cannot consent to do so at the cost of any such imputation on myself, and I therefore determined, in every instance, to name, or, at least to indicate the gentlemen, who were my companions and associates in the sports which I have described.

THE SEA-SERPENT

Who has not heard of the sea-serpent? There was no educated man in the United States, at least, who had not read with wonder, not unmixed with awe, of the visits of this formidable animal to the coasts of New England. Nothing could be better authenticated than the existence of this undescribed marine monster—nothing more circumstantial and truthlike than the statements published in the Boston papers of the visits made by the nondescript, to the vicinity of Gloucester Point and Nahant! We were told how it appeared on a certain day off Gloucester and was seen by two skippers commanding separate vessels—how it approached one of the sail, as if for the purpose of attack—how its eyes were fierce and fiery—how its head, large as a flour barrel, was raised three feet above the water—how its length was from 90 to 120 feet—how its back while it moved along presented the appearance of bunches which projected above the surface, and how, after approaching within fifty yards of the vessel, it dived beneath it and disappeared, to the unspeakable relief of the crew! It seemed impossible, from the mass of corroborative testimony, to question two important facts—first, the existence of this strange and formidable animal, and secondly, that it took the form of a serpent! It was no myth, but an actual, living, formidable, unchronicled monster of the deep; and, in the excited state of the public mind, expeditions were planned with a view to capture it, and put to rest all future incredulity, by exhibiting it to the gaze of the people.

I remember dining, during this excited state of the public mind, with Dr. Robbins of Boston, at his cottage at Nahant. I well remember the sumptuous fare spread before us by our hospitable host—the delicacy of the viands, the lusciousness of the fruits, the richness of the wines; but what I recall with more especial pleasure, is that Prescott the historian was among the guests, and charmed every stranger present by his colloquial powers, and by a modesty of deportment which sat on him too naturally to have been assumed. By my side, too, sat my early friend and cherished classmate, Francis C. Gray of Boston—now, alas! no more—the refined gentleman, the accomplished scholar, the keen, discriminating writer, whose unnumbered kindnesses come crowding thickly on my memory, as I recall his name—and dim my eyes while I write, with tears!

The cottage of Dr. Robbins was seated on the very cliff, and overlooked the sea. The cloth was hardly removed, when a murmuring noise from without induced us to look out, and we observed that the adjoining rocks were being fast populated by an anxious crowd, who were looking intently toward the sea; our eyes took the same direction—and there on the smooth surface, lay the sea-serpent! There

was the ripple, there were the bunches—just as they
had been described in print, there was the long *wake*,
leaving it uncertain what was the actual body,
and what represented the displacement of the water
caused by the rapid motion of the animal. An
excitement seized upon us all, and obeying an
impulse which my former training may well explain,
I resolved to volunteer with any party that should
attempt his capture. Meantime, the serpent disappeared, and when he next presented himself on the
surface we brought a telescope to bear on him, and
found to our infinite chagrin, that the object which
magnified by the haze of the atmosphere, had seemed
to us the veritable sea-serpent, had now shrunk to
the dimensions of a despicable horse-mackerel!

"But surely, sir, you have mistaken your latitude—you are adrift without a compass! What
have you to do with the sea-serpent? He is the
peculiar property of New England, he never con-
descends to show himself elsewhere, he is of the
Pilgrim States, their very specialty; as much and
as exclusively theirs, as the gift of witchcraft, the
privilege of detecting, and the divine right of
punishing it. With what propriety, therefore, can
you pretend to introduce him in a book of 'Carolina
Sports?'"

Have patience! most choleric reader! Patience
is a piscatory as well as an Apostolic virtue; as
needful (you may find) to the reader of fish stories,
as to the fisherman himself. Patience, and we shall
see.

7—C. S.

The March winds were whistling sharply, as is their wont, along the southern Atlantic sea-board, when the gallant steamer Wm. Seabrook loosed her hawser from the wharf at Savannah to which she had been moored, and pressed forward on her inland voyage to Charleston. At her wheel stood her stalwart commander, Blankinsop, long known and well reputed in all the region roundabout. And now the steamer glides through the yellow waters of the Savannah River, between fields celebrated for their production of rice, and enriched by the deposit from these same turbid yellow waters, until they rival Egypt in fertility. And well they may—for while only one annual inundation enriches the Egyptian soil, here, twice in the short life of every moon, are these fields refreshed and renewed by fertilizing inundations; and now the steamer approaches the sea, whose salt tides contend for mastery with the fresh waters from the high lands, that having long held undisputed possession of the channel, are now urging boisterously their exclusive and prescriptive right, against the encroachments of the ocean. And now she winds along the cork-screw channel—worn by the contending tides in the soft oozy bottom—and weathers the black-oyster rocks, and rounds the tail of Grenadier bank with its flankers of snow-white breakers, and then she bears up for Callibogue Sound, and passes the mouth of the river of "May"—Laudonnières' river of that name, or else wrongfully baptized in it, by

some bungling geographer; and then with rapid
strokes, she dashes through Skull Creek—Hilton
Head on the starboard, Pinckney Island on the lar-
board bow—till all at once she emerges on the broad,
deep estuary of Port Royal, already familiar to the
reader as the sporting ground and the battle ground
of the devil-fish! And now the steamer was merrily
dashing the foam from her prow—weathering the
tail of Paris bank, and pointing up Beaufort River
toward the town of that name, when lo and behold!
what startling spectacle then met the gaze of the
astonished commander! What but the veritable
sea-serpent! that tired, we may suppose, of the
monotony of his eastern haunts, was amusing himself with an excursion to the South, and had looked
in (*en passant*) on the pleasant harbor of Port
Royal! Mars and Bellona! what did the captain
do? There lay alongside of him this leviathan of
sea monsters, "long as his steamboat, stout as his
yawl." There he lay in his interminable length, his
bunches all visible (as may be seen on the frontis-
piece of many a veracious pamphlet of the day),
each several bunch of the series set down by
authority, and verified by a Gloucester affidavit!
What did the captain do? Why, like a prudent and
considerate commander, he did not do what you or
I, in a dare-devil spirit might have done—*he did
not* attack the monster! He would not risk owner's
property, you see! If he attacked the strange craft,
and came to damage thereby, he might forfeit insur-

ance, for this risk was not put down in the policy, you know! So, giving the monster a wide berth, he turned tail, blew off three terrific blasts at him from his steam whistle, and drove away for the town of Beaufort, as if the devil himself was in his rear!

The captain had no sooner reached the wharf, and disclosed his startling intelligence, than the whole town was aflame with excitement!

"What is this?" said a fine looking burly gentleman, who came bustling down with an air of official authority about him. "What hoax are you playing off on us? The sea-serpent in Broad River! Tell that to the marines!"

"As sure as you live," said the captain, "I saw him two hours ago."

"The hell you did! Why did you not hawser him, and bring him up to town?"

"He was as large round as my yawl boat, and as long as the steamer," said the captain, explanatorily.

"The old one, of course," said the stout gentleman. "But what should the devil or any of his vicegerents find to do in these waters? I should be glad to know! Didn't the Saints make such a clean sweep of us some years back, that devil a subject can now be found among us, fit for his majesty's service?"

"I don't know that," said a keen looking, ascetic man, in a quiet tone, "he might get some, from what I hear, by voluntary enlistment!"

"The captain took an afternoon observation," hinted one.

"Twilight magnifies," said another. But in spite of jeers and doubts, the captain's testimony was positive, earnest and unvarying, and the conviction soon became general that the monster was really in Port Royal! Then came the unanimous determination to capture him at all hazards!

"We'll teach this Yankee craft to cruise in our waters," said one.

"Doubtless, he has his belly stuffed with abolition tracts," said a hungry looking secessionist, leading off on the grateful scent.

"Gentlemen," said a third, "the sea-serpent is here—that's a fact. We must capture him, that's another fact, or soon will be. Who'll volunteer? He shall not insult us by his presence in these waters—us, who have encountered and beaten the devil-fish, who are his betters for aught we know—us, who have trailed behind them all night in our undecked skiff, on the open sea, and mastered them with the rising sun. We'll kill him, gentlemen; we're the boys to do it." And it was resolved!

The steamer whose intelligence had caused such unwonted commotion in this ordinarily tranquil town, now steamed off for her destination, unconscious of, and indifferent to, the ferment she had excited. Oh, Beaufort! thou mother of beautiful women and illustrious men, who devotest thy daughters to Heaven, in this world and the next; but

dismissest thy sons in an opposite direction! Thou
unmatchable town, that, devouring the oyster, still
delightest in the shell! Whose mansions, streets,
and roads, are all of shell-work; that blindest the
eyes of thy people with concrete dust, and with concrete walls defendest thyself against the approach
of thy enemies! Thou mathematical paradox, whose
angles become right lines by "order of council,"
and whose right lines are as tortuous as angles!
Thou financial wonder! whose taxes increase as thy
means diminish, and whose inhabitants grow rich
by borrowing from each other! Oh, Beaufort!
lovely always, but like a freckled beauty, loveliest
at a distance! what a storm of excitement burst over
you on this eventful night, and startled you from
your accustomed somnolency! There was many a
lovely eye that did not close a lid, for fear of the
encroachment of the serpent! There was many a
manly heart that waked as well, but throbbed with
impatience to grapple with, and subdue him! They
did not sleep; long before midnight the lieges of
Beaufort were afloat, intent on mischief. Prominent
among them was Capt. J. G. B., once the honored
captain of the Beaufort Volunteer Guards—now
the commander of the consolidated corps of artillery
and guards. He was to command the artillery of the
expedition. A man of honor and worth was he; a
high-toned man, whose only quarrel with life was,
that his military aspirations had never been gratified: that his misgoverned country had never

indulged in the luxury of war, nor afforded him the opportunity for that distinction, for which his soul pined! "Here is a chance after all," said the captain, rubbing his hands. "It is not war, but something almost as good!" Then there was Captain G. P. E., whilom captain of this same artillery. He was to command the squadron. Confident was he of making minced-meat of the sea-monster! "Had he not driven bayonets and pikes and harpoons innumerable into devil-fish? Was he to be daunted now? No, not he! He would draw the serpent's teeth, and leave them in pawn with his friend who swore so terribly! He would give his flesh to the sharks—his skeleton to Dr. ———, in exchange for a unicorn, or to his friend the colonel, in exchange for his favorite mermaid! His skin he would present to the museum at Salem, to be exhibited gratis to the enterprising people of Gloucester, and in exchange, if they could find one, for the skin of a witch."

They launched a flat, which, in consideration, doubtless, of his known antipathy to serpents, they dubbed "Saint Patrick," and in it embarked Captain B. with his six-pounder, well supplied with ammunition, and with a select squad of artillerists to serve it. Next came Captain G. P. E. in his sail boat, "The Eagle," with a lighter armament, but indorsed by an apparatus fitted for devil-fishing, such as harpoons, ropes, and buoys. Lastly, came a skiff, to ply between the heavier boats, and pick up stragglers should any be tossed overboard in the

expected fray. Here was good strategy—an anchor
to windward, a loop-hole for retreat, were it necessary, and security for some at least of the assailants,
for it would be difficult for his highness, with all his
imputed fierceness and voracity, to take down three
boats at a gulp!

Full of spirit, and of high hope and expectation,
the party now embarked, and went merrily on their
way with wind and tide in their favor, until at dawn
of day they found themselves on the waters of
Broad River, by the way of Archer's Creek. They
cast their eyes wistfully east, south and west, over
the wide expanse, but no serpent was to be seen.
They agreed to divide, and signal each other should
either party come in sight of the enemy. "St.
Patrick," with the skiff in company, passed up the
river with the tide (you are too fond of that, my
dear St. Patrick!) The Eagle spreads her wings
and sails away to seaward, against the tide. After
sailing on that tack for some time without seeing
anything unusual, she turns to rejoin her consort,
who had now made an interval of several miles
between the boats; when the look-out boy stationed
in the bow of the Eagle calls out, "I see something
ahead!" "Where?—where?" and all hands rush to
the head of the boat to see, and beheld close aboard
of them an object like a boat turned bottom up.
"Gentlemen," said Captain George, "look out, the
object is right ahead—but a hundred yards off—we
shall be in the jaws of the serpent before we can

stop! Helm down." The boat would not answer the helm, there was too much live weight at the bows. "To your places, gentlemen! Let go sheet ropes!" She fell off from the wind, and the boat passes, just without touching, the object which had called forth this sudden commotion. "Very like a whale," cried Captain George, as he gazed at the unknown. "Look there! another; we're in a shoal of whales! There's five of them, as I live; three full grown and two young ones! No sea-serpent, after all; but game, nevertheless, and royal game too; a perfect godsend to us—let us signal our consort, and bring them to action."

"Ah, Saint Patrick! that habit of yours, of taking it aisy, and going with wind and tide, has brought you into trouble! These four miles of head wind and tide, and hard tugging at the oars, before you can face the enemy, all come of this obliging disposition of yours!" The whales, too, were going against the tide, so that the match after all was not so very unequal, and St. Patrick, after a hard tug, with a swaggering air, that seemed to say, "arrah now, won't I take the consait out of you?" ranged up alongside the enemy, and when he had got within a hundred yards, let go a six-pound ball at the first whale that showed himself above the water. "They take no notice of us!" said the baffled artilleryman. "Try another shot." They tried another and another, but the balls went dancing and ricocheting over the waves innocent of blood! No wonder!

the wind blew high, the sea was rough, and Saint
Patrick (shame on him) was a leetle unsteady!
"Now, Slowman," said Captain B., "try your hand;
your father was our crack shot, and *you* boast that
you can bring down a sparrow on the wing with
your six-pounder; show us your skill, now!" "Well,
captain, but a sparrow on the wing is easier than a
whale under water; but here goes!" And he rams
down a canister of grape, and when the next whale
rises, a shower of balls is flying about his head.
"Ha, ha! he feels us now!" The whale flings his
fluke aloft, and brings it down on the water with a
report that rivalled our cannon, then plunges downward, and when he next shows himself on the surface, there are some keen-sighted sportsmen aboard
who aver that they spy a hole in his jacket, and a
piece of blubber fat sticking out of the orifice!

Meanwhile, the whales began to move at increased
speed toward the sea, and it became doubtful
whether St. Patrick could retain his position so as
to continue the action.

"Come," said Captain George, "they must not
escape us. I'll go in the skiff, and tackle them with
my devil-fish harpoon. Who'll steer the skiff? I'll
take two boys to row."

"But, maussa," said Pompey (who was one of the
skiff hands), "I can't go close dat ting in maussa
new boat anyhow. He tail strong as steam engine,
and he knock the boat all to shivers."

"Don't want you, Pompey; another hand will do as well, or better."

So off they start; Captain George, staff in hand, at the bow, while two hands pulled vigorously at the oars. The ripple caused by the motion of the fish against the current, showed their direction, even while they were submerged. So, rowing parallel to the shoal, the whale had no sooner emerged, than the boatmen were ordered to pull right in for his head. The boat actually touched him, when Captain George struck the harpoon into his head, and as he seemed stunned or insensible, drove it in with both hands, till the skiff recoiled with the force of the blow. Thirty fathoms of rope, attached to the harpoon, had been wound round a cask, which was now thrown overboard, and the cask began to spin around in a marvellous manner, until the whole line was unwound, when it went bobbing under and reappearing, with the rapid or slower movement of the fish.

Three cheers went up from the assembled sportsmen at the execution of this daring feat; and high hopes were entertained that they would succeed in capturing the whale. The fish, meanwhile, floundered and plunged, and lashed the water with his powerful fluke, whirling over while on the surface, until the rope was observed to be twisted several times round his body, while the staff was seen sticking from his throat. The sportsmen, in their three boats, followed closely in his wake, waiting for him to exhaust himself, and in the interim, betook themselves to breakfast. Suddenly, the cask became motionless. They approach, pull upon the line, and, to their deep mortification, discover that the harpoon had drawn out.

"Now is *my* turn," said Captain John; and, taking his place in the skiff, he repeated the exploit of Captain George—struck a fish with great force, which, like his predecessor, contrived, after a short struggle, to rid himself of the harpoon.

"My turn is come again," said Captain George; and, planting himself a second time in the bow of the skiff, he struck his harpoon deeply, this time, in the body of the fish. Again were witnessed the furious plunges and contortions of the whale; again the harpoon tore out, and the baffled sportsmen, on the failure of this, their third cast, had to confess to themselves, that their tackle was inadequate to the capture of a whale. The wind now veered to the east, and a rain-storm set in, so that it was necessary to draw off from the enemy, and make a harbor for the security of the boats, and especially of that which was burdened with a piece of artillery, which was accordingly done.

The next day was Sunday, and our sportsmen did not follow the example of the commanders of modern Christian armies, who apparently select that day for an engagement. They staid at home, and retook their positions on Monday, with better knowledge, better equipments, and in every way better prepared for success. But all too late—the enemy had fled! The captain of a coaster met them on their retreat, as they left the harbor; and nothing more was heard of them, except that rumor reported one of them as having been stranded on the island of Kiawah!

When, during the pursuit of these whales, the fish occasionally threw themselves in line, following in each other's wakes near the surface, with their fins projecting above the water, the close resemblance to an immense serpent was brought strikingly to the minds of our sportsmen; and it was easy to perceive, how, in a hazy atmosphere, or during an agitated sea, the sporting of a shoal of whales might represent (to the mind of an excited mariner), and be honestly mistaken for the redoubtable sea-serpent!

When the expedition returned to Beaufort, there were some to taunt it with its want of success.

"Well, Captain George, where is your prize? You have not caught the whale, after all."

"No," says Captain George, "but we have done better; we have killed the sea-serpent!"

" Three cheers went up from the assembled sportsmen at the execution of this daring feat. . . . The fish, meanwhile, floundered and plunged, and lashed the water with his powerful fluke."

DRUM FISHING

[P O G O N I A S   C H R O M I S.]

BEAUFORT, S. C.

MR. EDITOR: I comply with your request, that I would furnish you with some account of our favorite sport of "drum fishing," though I am aware that the detail will interest but a small portion of your readers.

These fish are so called, from the noise they make, resembling the tap of a drum, and so loud, that in calm weather and in the afternoon (which is their favorite time for *drumming*), it may be heard at the distance of several hundred yards from the river. They are known to frequent our waters during every month of the year except two, (December and January), yet it is only during the spawning season that they drum—at all other seasons they are mute— it is the universal passion alone that gives them utterance! It is only at this season, too, that they take the hook: at other times, they subsist on barnacles and oysters, sustaining themselves by a process called *grubbing*.

They are a numerous family, and make annual excursions along our coast from Florida as far north as the harbor of New York, where I have heard of a few having been taken. In the month of April, they abound on the sea-coast of South Carolina, and great numbers penetrate our inlets for the purpose of depositing their spawn. The large bay or sound, known on the maps as Port Royal harbor, but locally, as *Broad River*, is their chosen place of resort, and constitutes the best fishing station. If you ask me *why* they give the preference to this particular spot, I answer you conjecturally—because, while it is the deepest and most capacious bay along our whole southern coast, it is at the same time the saltest, there being no important streams from the interior, emptying themselves into it and neutralizing the properties of the sea-water.

But many of your readers, Mr. Editor, have never seen a drum-fish. It may be proper, therefore, for me to state, that it is the largest *scale* fish in America. It measures ordinarily three feet in length, and weighs from thirty to forty pounds. It is beautifully marked on the sides, by broad dark transverse stripes, alternating with silver—or else exhibits a uniform bright gold color, which fades, soon after it is taken, into the hues already described. I give you the *medium* weight and size of the fish, not the extreme. I have taken one which measured four feet six inches in length and weighed eighty-five pounds. Out of twenty taken by me on a particular day, during the present season (April), there were three weighing from sixty-five to seventy pounds each. The smaller-sized fish are excellent for table use—their roes, especially, are a great

delicacy; the larger are only valuable when salted
and cured like cod-fish, from which when dressed
they are scarcely distinguishable in flavor. The
planters of this vicinity are skillful fishermen and
much devoted to the sport. They succeeded in
taking, during the last season, at least twelve thousand of these fish; and when I add, that except the
small number consumed in their families, the
remainder were salted and distributed among their
slaves, not in lieu of, but in addition to their
ordinary subsistence, you will perceive that this is a
case wherein the love of sport, and the practice of
charity, are singularly coincident.

And now, for the manner of taking them. The
sportsman must provide himself with a substantial
boat impelled both by oars and sail, and with at
least fifteen fathoms of rope to his grapnel. His
line must be thirty fathoms, and furnished with two
pounds of lead, distributed in movable sinkers,
which draw up or let down, according to the strength
of the tide. He must lay in a good stock of crabs,
clams, and prawns, for bait; and having launched
his boat on the bosom of this beautiful bay, and
come to anchor in about five or six fathoms water,
on gravelly or rocky bottom, he has now done
everything which can be considered as prerequisite
to a successful fishing. Having baited his hook
with either or with a mixture of these different
baits, (the prawn, though thirty years ago unknown
as a bait for drum, are decidedly the best), let out

your line until it keeps the bottom, and stand prepared for a bite! The unpractised sportsman, who supposes that their bite will be in proportion to their size and strength, will draw up many a naked hook, before he draws a fish. They approach cautiously, and almost as if they expected a snare. As soon as you feel him certainly at your hook, jerk with your utmost strength, and draw quickly upon him, until you have fixed the hook in his jaws. The instant he feels the smart he dashes off with all his force: and this is the critical moment—for if you resist him too forcibly, he breaks your tackle, or tears out your hook! and if you give him slack line, he darts toward you, and shakes the hook out of his mouth. "A just medium," as Sterne says, "prevents all conclusions." *In medio, tutissmus ibis.* You must give him play, keeping your line tight, yet not overstrained; preserving an equable pressure; managing your line with one hand, and keeping the other in reserve, either to draw in rapidly when the run is toward you, or to regulate the velocity when the run is against you, and severe. By degrees, the efforts of the fish relax, and he is drawn to the surface. At the sight of the sun, he makes a final effort to escape, and plunges till he has reached the bottom. The fatal hook still adheres to his jaws, and when he reappears exhausted, on the surface of the water, it is only to turn on his back, and resign himself to his fate. A barbed iron, fastened to a wooden staff, is then struck into him, and you lift

8—C. S.

your prize into the boat. Generally speaking, you
are occupied five minutes in taking a fish; but if the
tide be strong, and the fish large, your sport may
last fifteen.

There is great uncertainty attending this sport;
the patience of the fisherman may be severely tested;
sometimes you have the mortification to hear them
drumming beneath your boat, while they stubbornly
refuse to be taken—rejecting untasted the most
tempting baits you can offer; at other times they are
in better humor. As a general rule, with five lines
in your boat, you may count on fifteen or twenty fish
as the result of a day's sport. Occasionally, you
have memorable luck—sixty-three were taken during
the present season, by a boat with seven lines, and I
once knew a boat with ten lines to take as many as
ninety-six; the best success I have met with, personally, was to take forty, to three lines—eighteen
fish fell to my share of the sport; my two oarsmen
took the remainder. *Thirty* fish were all that the
boat could conveniently contain; her gunwale was
but a few inches above the water, and we slung the
ten (which were *de trop*) alongside, by a rope. In
this situation we were attacked by sharks. These
"grim companions," would range up alongside, and
make a rush at them to cut them off; and we were
compelled to beat them off with boat-hooks. A little
more boldness in their attack, and we must have
fallen victims; for a single blow from their tails
would have filled our overloaded boat. As it hap-

pened we were unattended by any other boat which
could have rendered assistance, and were full three
miles from shore. In the sport of this day, my
gloves were torn into shreds by the friction of the
line, and my fingers so blistered by the severity of
the play that I was incapable of renewing my sport
for several days.

I love all sports, whether "by flood or field," and
have engaged in many an animating scene of sylvan
and aquatic amusement; but I have found none,
devil-fishing alone excepted, possessed of so absorbing an interest as *successful* drum-fishing. Imagine
yourself afloat on our beautiful bay, the ocean before
you, the islands encircling you, and a fleet of forty
or fifty fishing boats (their white awnings glistening
in the sun) riding sociably around. Suddenly, a
school of fish strike at some particular boat; a
second is engaged—the direction of the school is
indicated—the boats out of the run of the fish, draw
up their anchors and place themselves rapidly alongside, or in the rear of the successful boats, and soon
they participate in the sport; and now two, three,
a dozen, nay, twenty boats, are engaged; in some
boats, three at a time are drawn alongside—the fish
dart across each other—the lines are entangled—the
water foams with the lashing of their tails, and the
fisherman scarce knows, while they flounder on the
surface, which fish belongs to his own hook, which
to his neighbors; the barb is dashed hurriedly and
at random into the yet struggling fish—and each

one is burning with anxiety to secure his fish and
return to the sport, before the favorable moment has
passed. The interest is intense. Isaac Walton knew
nothing like this—if he had, he must have disdained
all smaller fry—and have abandoned the impaling
of minnows, and the enticement of trouts, to indulge
in the superior pleasure of drum-fishing.

PISCATOR.

BASS FISHING

Not less certain in its periodical visit to our coast, than the drum, is that beautiful sea-fish, the bass—though the time of its advent is October, instead of April. Yet, as they give no warning of their visit by *sound*, the fact of their presence is not so well known, and they are, therefore, less persecuted by the fishermen. I do not mean the sea-bass of New York (our black-fish)—Centropristes Nigricans—nor yet the striped bass, taken among the rocks at Newport (our rock-fish)—Labrax lineatus—this fish, in very fine condition, is taken at the South in the *fresh water* rivers; but *the bass* par excellence—*Corvina oscellata*—weighing thirty or forty pounds, three feet and upward in length, elegantly shaped, brilliant with silvery and golden hues, and distinguished by one or more dark black spots upon the tail.

The tackle and equipments required for taking them are much the same as those used for drum fishing—but your range of bait is greater; for while the drum refuses all except the shrimp and the shell-fish tribes, the bass will take, in addition, and with even more readiness, the skip-jack and the mullet. They are bold biters, and give the sportsman fair notice of their presence. Their mouths are hard and bony, and they sometimes escape by crushing

the hook. They run with such vivacity, that though
weighing less than the drum, they give you nearly
as much resistance in the capture. An iron gaff
is used to lift them on board. They are taken in the
greatest number from the 10th to the 20th October.
They ascend the branches of Port Royal Sound for
fifteen or twenty miles, but are found most numerous
immediately about the mouth. They either feed
along the shallows in the surf, or frequent the deep
rocky channels of the river. In Daws' Channel,
there is frequently good fishing. But greater sport
has been had on what are termed the Bay Point
rocks, than on any other spot within the inlet. The
headlands, which, a few miles above, are separated
by an expanse of eight or ten miles of water,
approach each other at this point within four miles;
and the tide water consequently rushes with great
force through this gorge. The sand has been swept
away, and the rocky bed of the river exposed by
this action of the water; but the rock being of
unequal hardness, is unequally worn; and the more
enduring portions jut out from below, in irregular
masses, amidst whose crags and crannies the sea-
weeds grow, and shell-fish congregate. To these
spots, therefore, the larger fish repair for subsistence. The skill of the sportsman is exerted in hit-
ting one of these detached masses, which are separated many yards apart; and his sport depends
upon the accuracy with which he takes his drop.
Let him row over from Bay Point toward the Hilton

Head shore—putting the last hammock,* on the southwestern end of Eddings' Island, in line with the most northwardly point of the same island; and extend the chord of this arc, until he opens the first woods of Chaplin's Island, beyond the Bay Point beach. Dropping his anchor at the precise intersection of these two lines, he has the best ground probably in the whole southern country; where he may, in their proper season, take black-fish, sheepshead, bass and drum in abundance, and, occasionally, *all of them on the same day.*

A third line was formerly drawn in confirmation of the above; it was by placing the last pines on the Hilton Head beach in range with the mansion-house of Gen. C. C. Pinckney, on Pinckney Island. But this mansion no longer exists; it was swept away in one of the fearful hurricanes that vex our coast! To this spot, that sterling patriot and lion-hearted soldier retired from the arena of political strife, to spend the evening of his days in social enjoyment and literary relaxation. On a small island, attached to the larger one, which bears his name, and which, jutting out into the bay, afforded a delightful view of the ocean, he fixed his residence! *There,* in the midst of forests of oak, laurel and palmetto, the growth of centuries, his mansion-house was erected. There stood the laboratory, with its apparatus for chemical experiments—the

---

*An umbrella-shaped cedar now marks the spot.

library, stored with works of science in various tongues; there bloomed the nursery for exotics; and there was found each other appliance with which taste and intelligence surround the abodes of wealth. It is melancholy to reflect on the utter destruction that followed; even before the venerable proprietor had been gathered to his fathers! The ocean swallowed up everything; and it is literally true, that the sea monster now flaps his wings over the very spot where his hearth-stone was placed—where the rites of an elegant hospitality were so unstintedly dispensed—and where the delighted guest listened to many an instructive anecdote, and unrecorded yet significant incident of the revolutionary period, as they flowed from the cheerful lips of the patriot. It argues no defect of judgment in Gen. Pinckney, that he lavished such expense on a situation thus exposed. In strong practical sense he was surpassed by no man. It was, in truth, his characteristic. He built where trees of a century's growth gave promise of stability; but in our southern Atlantic borders, he who builds strongest does not build on rock—for among the shifting sands of our coast, old channels are closed, and new ones worn, by the prevailing winds and currents, through which the waters are poured, during the storms of the equinox, with a force that nothing can resist.

We will suppose that the sportsman has hit the precise spot, and is riding quietly at anchor in six fathoms water, above one of these populous thoroughfares of the scaly nations. His success soon excites the attention of the surrounding sportsmen. They approach, modestly at first, and drop alongside at thirty yards' distance—then gradually nearer, till ten yards' space does not separate the boats—still without success; while the more fortunate fisherman is satiated with sport! Some drop behind, and some, perhaps, with an awkward apology for violating the courtesy of the river, drop directly ahead. It makes no difference—one boat has all the play. "What bait have you? Very strange!—ours is just the same! Never saw anything so provoking in my life. You have the devil's luck, and that's the truth." And some, more touchy and petulant than the rest, move off to more distant grounds, where they escape, at least, the pain of witnessing a success that they cannot share. More than once have I found myself in this envied, but unenviable position. I like my full share, I confess, but not the monopoly of the sport; and, on one occasion, I remember to have invited alongside, one of my neighbors, who looked particularly chagrined at his comparative want of success. "Come alongside," said I, "and I will explain this matter to you. You are aware that much depends on the *drop*. You have no success; you are only taking the stragglers, as it were, who are traversing the bye-lanes below—while I am over the banqueting house! Now, observe, my anchor is fast

to a crag below. I have a buoy to the end of the
rope; at still-tide it rises to the surface, when I
attach my boat to it, and thus secure my drop.
Now, I have taken as many fish as I wish, and
am about to cast off my rope—receive it in your
boat, and you will succeed to my good-fortune."
With this slight change of position, came a change
of luck; and I had the satisfaction, while I sailed
away from the ground, to see him merrily engaged
in the sport.

The accuracy with which, in an inlet so wide and
deep (and with no other guides than trees and landmarks, distant from four to eight miles), the drop
is taken, is matter of frequent surprise. For example,
my rope parted in a hard blow, and my anchor
remained at the bottom. I fished it up five years
afterward, drawing up the old anchor on the fluke
of the new—and identified it by the covering of
sheet lead which I had wrapped round the shank
to increase its weight. Still more remarkable is the
fact I am about to record. It is one of those cases,
sometimes occurring, in which fact seems stranger
than fiction!

I was fishing in October, 1841, on Bay Point
rocks, for bass. Nathl. Heyward, Jun., and my
young son, nine years of age, were in the boat with
me. My son sat on my left, and fastened his line
to a rock, as he thought, below. "But see," said
he, "I can draw it up some feet from the bottom." I
felt it, and it swayed a few feet, but would come

no further; and I concluded he had struck his hook into a fragment of rope attached to some lost anchor. Nothing remained but to pull upon it; when the line came up, minus the hook, which remained, with the strap attached, fixed in the object below. *We drew up anchor, and returned to the shore on the ebb tide to dinner*, but having had very good sport, determined to resume our drop on the afternoon tide. Now, it almost exceeds belief to state—what is nevertheless absolutely true—that the drop was resumed with such extreme accuracy, that my son, sitting again on my left hand, fastened his line a second time to the same obstruction below; and drew up on his hook, the self-same hook which he had lost in the morning—identified beyond all question, *by the strap attached to it!* The chances were a million to one against such precision in taking the drop; yet, as there are three living witnesses to these facts, I shall not hesitate to record them, however improbable they may appear.

Three or four miles to the south and east of these rocks lies Joyner's Bank; separated from the Gaskin by a swash of five fathoms water. Not more than a fathom and a half is found on the crown of the ridge, which subsides rapidly on the north into the deep channel. The ebb-tide rushes over this bank with great force, and makes a very distinct ripple, which marks its location. The shrimps and smaller fry are pursued, when passing this ridge, by the

skip-jacks; and they, in turn, by the bass and
sharks; while the sea-gulls hover screaming above,
and dip into the water, whenever their prey, driven
from below by hosts of enemies, approaches near
enough to the surface to be seized in their beaks!
You anchor your boat on the tideward side of the
ridge, so as to let your line lead into the ripples;
and there you may enjoy memorable sport. Nothing, indeed, can exceed it, when the bass are
assembled in force. Once or twice, I have found
them in such numbers that the bottom seemed paved
with them. It was thus at my first visit to Joyner's
Bank. It was sufficient to get your line overboard
to insure a bite; but, in fifteen minutes, the boat was
in a state of "most admired disorder"—the bottom
covered with these fish, all alive, and floundering
about with an energy now quite misplaced—the
boatmen leaping up on the thwarts, to escape a lick
upon their sensitive shins—the bait-basket knocked
overboard—the hooks snapped off and lost—and
the lines of all the sportsmen tangled and knotted
together in one web of inextricable confusion!

We retired from the ground, after having taken
five sharks and thirty-five bass; and we reproached
ourselves for not having doubled our success!—but
the truth was, we did not use our opportunities to
the best advantage—the sport was so exciting, that
we forgot our skill in our enjoyment. The best fishing I have known on this ground, comprised one
hundred and twenty bass, taken in one day, by three
boats fishing in company.

To improve the day to the uttermost in this sport, the fisherman must drop, on the morning high water, at the Bay Point rocks (for the fish bite best on these rocks at slack tide). When the ebb runs too hard to allow of his fishing longer on that ground, he must drop down to Joyner's Bank (the bass bite best there on the high ebb). On the early flood, he may take a few more by crossing the bank and dropping on the seaward side of the ridge; and then, on his way back, by anchoring on the flats of Egg Bank, as near to the breakers as he safely can, and tossing his line into the surf, he may complete the round of his success.

The mention of Egg Bank reminds me that there is another mode of taking bass, which, to say the truth, I have not pursued much of late. This bank lies, or, more properly speaking, did lie, south of the public lot at Bay Point—distant half a mile. Covering several acres in extent, and lifting its head a few feet above high-water mark, it served as the secure roosting place of the curlews, sea-gulls, and other aquatic birds; and here, too, in the spring, they deposited their eggs. But the hurricanes which periodically sweep along our coasts have so obliterated it, that its existence as an egg bank will become, in a few years, a matter of tradition. It is now covered at half flood—and its site is marked in stormy weather by the waves, that, rushing together from opposite quarters, meet at its summit, and, jutting upward into the air, fall in a

sheet of foam. When the bank stood above water,
it formed a barrier against the sea; and while the
surf beat on the outer side, the inner was protected,
so that a boat could land in security. I used to
push over from Bay Point at early flood, land on
the inner side of the bank, and, leaving a few oarsmen to take charge of the boat, walk over to the
sea-side of the bank, with a servant or two to carry
bait and lines; and, wading out into the surf waist-
deep, toss my line into the breakers in quest of
bass. I was usually armed with a light spear; for,
as the clear, transparent wave came rolling in from
the deep, and as the pearly fragments of sea-shell
passed glittering by you with the flux and reflux of
the tide, objects were occasionally encountered, as
brilliant, perhaps, but by no means as pleasant to
look upon: the eyes and jagged spines of immense
sting-rays, buried in the sand, all to these, and
lying in wait for their prey! One incautious step,
and your leg may be transfixed by the venomed
weapon! Sometimes, indeed, the bass would
approach close to your feet, in couples, and gaze
upon you, seemingly, with curiosity and alarm!
You might perceive their pectoral fins in rapid
play, as if they panted; while, at the lightest movement of your arm to hurl your spear, they vanished
in an instant, and left your weapon buried innocently in the sand. On one delightful day, I was
tempted to wade deeper than usual into the sea,
which was beautifully clear. I passed along the

narrow ridge of a reef, which extended eastwardly to a considerable distance from the main bank, while a swash of some depth lay close within. I had unconsciouss1y remained, until the advancing tide had covered the highest parts of the ridge full waist-deep. Behind me stood my servant "Cain," with my spear and a wicker-basket of bait. An exclamation of terror from him made me turn, when I beheld, but a few yards distant, between us and the shore, and intercepting our retreat, a large shark, close on the side of the ridge, head on for us, and waving his tail backward and forward with a deliberate sculling motion! "My spear," said I; "keep close to me, and shout when I do." "Great God," said Cain (his eyes almost starting from their sockets), "another one!" I looked, and saw, *not one, but two other sharks*, lying behind the first, all in a line, and in the same attitude! Doubtless the bait in the wicker-basket had attracted them; the advancing tide had carried them the scent, and these grim pointers had paused to reconnoitre, before they rushed on their prey. If they attacked *us*, we were gone! Not a moment was to be lost. It was one of those frequent cases, in which we find safety in audacity. Repeating my order to Cain, and grasping my spear in both hands, I rushed upon the leading shark, and struck it down violently across his nose—shouting, at the some time, at the top of my voice—while Cain, in a perfect agony of fear, gave a loud yell, and fell at full length in the water! The manœuvre succeeded; the sharks ran off for deep water, and we took the crown of the ridge, nor looked back, until we had accomplished the one hundred and fifty yards over which we had to wade before we regained the bank!

To be devoured by sharks, is one of the last deaths that I should choose. At this distance of time, I do not think of the adventure without a shudder. The sea is still as transparent as on that day, the sea-shells still as bright, the graceful bass still pants as he glides doubtingly by; but these things tempt me not to renew my sport. My mind reverts to other objects: the jagged barb of the sting-ray, lying in wait for his prey, and the outstretched jaws of the all-devouring shark, in which I had so narrowly escaped being engulfed! Who can endure the thought of being sepulchred in the "maw and gulf of the rav'ning salt-sea shark?" Not I!—I speak it in all sincerity. This was *my* last essay—and I henceforth leave to younger and more adventurous sportsmen—the pleasures and perils of *bass-fishing in the surf!*

SHEEPSHEAD FISHING

On the subject of sheepshead, I shall be brief, since there are few whose curiosity shall lead them to peruse these pages, who have not, either as fishermen or gastronomes, a familiar acquaintance with them. They are spread along our coast, from Florida to New York; but they who taste them at our great marts of business, after they have been captured at some distant point, and shut up, during a sea voyage, in the well of a smack, can have little understanding of their true culinary value. They should be eaten fresh; and, when boiled or broiled, are surpassed in flavor only by the cavalley—which holds the same rank among sea-fish, that the salmon does among those which inhabit the rivers. The drum and bass, on the contrary, are to be dressed in steaks, cut crosswise, and fried; and I may be forgiven, perhaps, for adding, that a grating of nutmeg sprinkled over them, before they are laid in the pan, has been deemed, by discriminating palates, to add richness to the flavor. But we anticipate: the old and approved formula says, "first catch your fish before you cook it,"—and we shall proceed, in due order, to do as it directs.

They are exceedingly choice in their feeding—taking no bait but shell-fish. Their favorite food is the young oyster, which, under the form of barnacle,

9—C.

they crush with their strong teeth. Of course, they
frequent those shores that abound with fallen trees.
On the Florida coast, they are taken in great quantities among the mangrove-trees, whose roots, growing in the salt water, are covered with barnacles.
Formerly, they were taken in considerable numbers
among our various inlets. Wherever there were
steep bluffs, from which large trees had fallen in
the water, there they might confidently be sought.
But as these lands have been cleared for the culture
of sea-island cotton, the trees have disappeared, and
with them the fish; and it has been found necessary
to renew their feeding-grounds by artificial means.
Logs of pine or oak are cut, and framed into a sort
of hut, without a roof. It is floored, and built up
five or six feet high; then floated to the place
desired and sunk in eight feet of water, by casting
stones or live-oak timber within. As soon as the
barnacles are formed, which will happen in a few
weeks, the fish will begin to resort to the ground.
It is sometimes requisite to do more, before you can
succeed in your wishes. The greatest enemies of
this fish are the sharks and porpoises—which pursue
them incessantly, and destroy them, unless they can
find secure hiding-places to which to retreat. Two
of these pens, near each other, will furnish this protection; and when that course is not adopted, piles
driven near each other, quite surrounding the pen,
will have the same effect. Your work complete,
build a light staging, by driving down four upright

posts, at a distance of fifteen feet from the pen; and
then take your station on it, provided with a light,
flexible and strong cane reed, of twenty feet length,
with fourteen feet of line attached—a strong hook,
and a light lead. Instead of dropping your line
directly down, and poising it occasionally from bottom, I prefer to throw the line out beyond the per-
pendicular, and let the lead lie on the bottom. The
sheepshead is a shy fish, and takes the bait more
confidently if it lies on the bottom. When he bites,
you perceive your rod dipping for the water—give
a short, quick jerk, and then play him at your
leisure. If the fish is large, and your jerk too violent, the rod will snap at the fulcrum—the grasp of
your left hand. It has happened that, at one of
these artificial grounds, I have taken sixteen sheepshead at one fishing. What was unusual, was, that
they were taken in February, when no one thinks
of fishing for these or any other sea-fish within the
inlets! I ascertained, from the continued experiments of several years, that they could always be
taken at this season, and frequently in January
also. The difficulty is to find bait, for neither
shrimps nor crabs are then in season. In the case
referred to, the difficulty was thus removed—the
lines were rigged with two hooks; upon one was
placed an oyster, taken fresh from the shell—on the
other, an oyster boiled. The scent of the first
attracted the fish; but so little tenacity was found
in it, that before the fish had taken hold of the hook,

the oyster was detached; but when, encouraged by
the taste of the first, the fish advanced to the second,
that having acquired toughness from boiling, would
adhere until the hook was fairly taken into the fish's
mouth. They clearly prefer the uncooked to the
cooked oyster; but the latter was more to the fisherman's purpose. Their fondness for this food
suggested the expedient of breaking up the live
oysters in the shell, and scattering them in the
vicinity of the ground; also that of letting down
the broken oysters in a wicker basket. Each plan
is found effectual in attracting the fish.

The bluffs, in their primitive state, in which trees
enough are found fallen, to give the fish both food
and protection against their enemies, are only to be
met with, now, among the hunting islands, where
the barrenness of the land had secured them against
cultivation. On two occasions, I have enjoyed
excellent sport at such places. On one I took
twenty-three to my own rod; on another, twenty-
four—and desisted from fatigue and satiety. They
are never taken in such numbers, when fishing from
a boat with a drop line, on the rocks. It is very
rare, that as many as twenty are taken in one boat.

About two hundred yards west by south from the
"Bay Point rocks," as already laid down under the
head of "Bass fishing," the rocky bed of the river
seems to be traversed by deep fissures, in which not
only the hooks of the fishermen are fixed, but the
anchors likewise. Though these have their ropes

fixed with a trip in view of such contingencies, they
are frequently, nevertheless, so fastened, that they
cannot be extricated. In these crannies are sheltered, besides the black-fish and sheepshead, the
overgrown toad-fish (the sculpin of the South),
eels of an immense size, and another fish, which
I shall describe, and whose name I would willingly add, were I able. I was fishing for bass in
1840, on this drop. My oarsman, next the bow,
was furnished with a shark line, with a chain hook,
for the accommodation of such large-sized sharks, as
it was not pleasant to have attached to a bass line.
He hooked, as he supposed, a shark, and after playing it for some minutes, called to me that it was
coming up. I hurriedly caught up the spear, and
transfixed, not a shark—but an enormous scale-
fish, of a description I had never seen before. With
the aid of the gaff and a loop, we hoisted him
on board, and I shortly after made for Bay Point
with my prize. Its shape was nearly that of the
fresh-water perch—known by the name of "wide-
mouthed perch"—which, by the way, my friend,
Professor Holbrook, says, is no perch at all, but a
"pomotis." Its hue was a greenish black on the
back, subsiding into a faint yellow on the belly;
its mouth was unfurnished with teeth, but had
slender spikes instead, with which it could hold
its prey; its eyes were large and prominent; its tail
was large at its insertion, and the paddle (caudal
rays) small in proportion to the size of the fish. It

resembled, in fine, an inhabitant of the fresh water, rather than the sea; was manifestly a heavy and dull swimmer; and it struck me as matter of surprise, that a fish thus formed, could escape for a day being destroyed by the sharks. I could only solve the difficulty, by supposing that he was born and bred among these rocks—the crevices of which had sheltered him from their attacks.

Desiring to show so uncommon a fish to the good people of Beaufort, I dispatched it thither in my boat, with a letter to a friend, requesting that he would have it accurately weighed and measured, and obtain from the savans of the place a scientific description; to facilitate which, I referred him to the books on natural history in the public library! My boat returned with a letter, *but without the fish.* It stated, in substance, "that the fish measured four feet eight inches in length; four feet eight inches in girth, and weighed one hundred and forty pounds; that the oldest sea-captain in the town had seen nothing like it; and that the scientific gentlemen who had examined it, could make nothing of it, except when brought on table—when they had enjoyed it exceedingly." So that the account of the fish might stand thus: "Length, 4 feet, 8 inches; girth, 4 feet, 8 inches; weight, 140 lbs. Scientific description.—'Devilish fine eating; sorry we could not spare you a slice.'"

"Well, my lad," said I to long Jeoffrey, who had taken the fish, and was not a little proud of it, "what has become of your fish?"

"Great massey, dey eat him up, and nebber gee me a taste!—so berry fat too!"

I had no Ariel at command to enter the conclave, where these sons of science sat in inquest on this extraordinary fish. I am obliged to sketch from fancy. The nondescript lies before them; his weight and measurement have been taken; and ejaculations of wonderment duly exchanged. Dr. Pogonias presides; and a few leaves of the books of reference, that are spread upon the table, have been turned— when the first incision, to test the internal structure, was made. The knife glides without effort through the tender fibre—the coats are lined with luscious-looking fat, and, on further investigation, two fresh sheepsheads—(Ha! ha! gentle reader!—you thought you caught me napping *but it is a sheepshead story, after all*—though you could not guess how I was to get at it)—two sheepsheads, fresh and bright and intact, are disclosed, on which he had made his morning lunch? A momentary frown passes over the brow of one of the pannel, as if he rebuked, in spirit, the extravagant epicurism of the defunct. The books are closed—a new direction has evidently been given to their thoughts. "I wonder," says Dr. P., "whether the copper banks are anywhere nigh? Really, if I wasn't afraid of being poisoned, by eating an unknown fish, I should indeed venture to try a little of it." Whereupon, he ordered Jeoffrey (my quasi-Ariel) to cut off a little slice of twenty pounds, and transfer it to his kitchen. The contagion spread—the steel gleamed on every side—and, in the twinkling of an eye, the fish was dismembered and divided, like another Poland!

It was devoured with a gusto so absorbing, as to overwhelm all thoughts of science; and not even the skeleton of this mammoth perch remains, to be transferred to the shelves of a museum, in token of the truth of my story!

I might add to these sketches and descriptions, some account of the fishing in our fresh water lakes and rivers, but the readers of Walton and Cotton can, on this head, need no instruction from me. To say the truth, I am far less skilled in such fishing, having never resorted to it, except when the more exciting sport of sea-fishing could not he had— neither should I be insensible to the ridicule of beginning with a devil-fish, and ending with a minnow!

NOTE.—If a still better reason were wanted, why I should refrain from entering on this field, I should find it in the fact, that I should, in so doing, be forestalling public attention—be poaching, as it were, in a neighbor's preserve!—for the fish of our southern country, whether in lake, river, or sea, are already in the hands of Professor Holbrook; in whose elaborate work, shortly to be published, the man of science will find them classified and arranged in their *families*, *genera*, and *species*, while the general reader will be interested in their *habits*, and look with gratification on their *living images*, from the pencil of the skillful artist now engaged in their delineation.

SPORTS OF THE FIELD

A WILD-CAT HUNT IN CAROLINA

It is a pleasant thing to dash along with the throng, in an animated hunt; and it is pleasant, when the hunt is at an end, to fight the battle over with the companions of our sport; while the incidents, yet fresh, come pictured back to us, through the medium of the sparkling glass. But it is a cold thing, to tell over the same incidents to an unexcited third party; and a difficult thing, where a word too little makes you vague, and a word too much makes you tedious—so to tell them as to make your story please. Yet, if these scruples were to govern us, no sportsman would write—and none through our wide-spread country would know what his brother sportsman was about. For my reader's sake, I would desire to introduce him to some more exciting chase—but I trace no fancy sketch: and as a panther is not at my command, I must take him, without further preface, on a wild-cat hunt in South Carolina.

At eight o'clock, on a fine morning in February, we mounted our hunters, and pushed off for a cover, three miles distant from the town of Beaufort, where we expected to put up a cat. The field consisted of three veterans—Judge P., Doctor E., and myself, and two neophites, Splash and Dash. Two drivers, one mounted, and one on foot, managed

the dogs and beat the thickets. Four couple of
staunch hounds skirted the cover, while three pointers and a setter penetrated the thicket, and gave
variety to the sport, by springing occasionally a
woodcock, snipe or partridge, which we shot—*if
they came in our way.* Our guns, charged, the one
barrel with buck or duck and the other with bird
shot, kept us prepared for whatever game might
present itself.

The hounds had not long entered the thicket, in
which (from finding at its edge the remains of a
half-devoured rabbit) we concluded that the cat
still lurked, when they struck off on an animated
drag; and soon, a burst from the pack assured us
that the cat was roused. In a minute, the thicket
is surrounded—each hunter, as the cry approached
him poising his gun and peering into the tangled
copse to catch a glimpse of the fugitive. But he
keeps the cover, which is so thick as to defy the
keenest sight; and circles it securely, leaving the
dogs to tear their way through the briers. "Ha!
what is that? a shot!—another!" It is Splash, who
caught him peeping out of the thicket, and cracked
off his double barrel! "What news?" "Habet,"
says Splash. "Aye! we shall see," thought I, as
the dogs came sweeping by the spot, and made no
check in their career. "Another! what is that?"
It is the judge. "A sentence, is it not?" No!
the hounds yet fly with renovated speed, and more
animated cry. But what trampling noise is that?

It is the judge's steed, that, alarmed by this unwonted extra-judicial proceeding, has left his bridle dangling from the haw-tree, and pushed off might and main for the quiet of his stable at home. Let him go—"the hunt will not pause!" The driver is dismounted—the judge bestrides a new steed, and sits again prepared for mischief. Another shot! It is the doctor. *That prescription must tell!* No! not dead yet!—sure "he bears a charmed life!" Again, the hounds lead off; fiercer and shriller is their yell. Another shot! ah, now they pause—one savage growl—one stifled cry—and all is hushed. It is Dash, who, pouring his charge full in his throat, has given him his "coup de grâce."

It was a tall, gaunt he-cat, of twenty-five pounds weight; and while the hunters gathered round him, and drew him from the gripe of the dogs—

"How now?" says the judge, "what hocus pocus is here? This is a tawny, leopard-like animal, while I pronounce the cat I fired at to be bigger and blacker; I saw it clearly as it rolled over in the swamp at the flash of my gun."

"My opinion, in this case, is precisely the same," said the doctor. "I fired at a black cat; the dogs must have changed cats during the chase!"

"So much the better, gentlemen," said I; "we shall then have two cats, instead of one. Put on the hounds, boys!"

They were taken to the point from which the doctor fired; but the stupid animals could find no trail, but that which led them again to the spot on which the tawny cat lay dead!

"A new trial!" said the judge.

It was granted. The dogs are now led to the spot from which the judge fired. The issue is fairly made; but the canine jury return the same verdict.

"Confusion!" says the judge; "must I doubt my own eyes?"

The sequel shows, that it is safer to doubt our own senses, than the instinct of a hound; and that *his* inferences from the nose, are less fallible than those from human sight; for the cat, being duly subjected to a post-mortem examination, was found to have been struck by four out of the six shots fired at him—and the doctor's shot, of peculiar size, being lodged in his body, left no doubt of the fact, that the black cat of the doctor and judge was no other than the tawny cat of the rest of the field. Whether the change of color was in the skin of the cat, or the eye of the sportsman, or the distribution of light, we leave philosophers to determine—and proceed with our hunt.

Having admired, a while, the sharp claws and formidable fangs of our victim, his flat head, and ample development of the organ of destructiveness; and listened, with becoming interest, to the rapid sketch which each sportsman successively gave of his own share in the death, we slung our cat upon the fork of an oak, to wait our return, and pushed on to beat another thicket. But here, either there was no cat; or, if there was, he had ensconced himself behind an intrenchment of briers, which hounds, unless their blood was heated by pursuit, would not willingly enter—so that he remained undetected.

And now the hunt, like our story, was in danger of flagging for want of incident: for there was little to rouse us, except when, at long intervals, a shot was fired at a partridge, that went whirring along before us, or a rabbit that imprudently broke cover, till at last we reached a gall, the thickest and most impenetrable to be found in all that region, and which, it was easy to perceive, must furnish a favorite lurking place for a cat. We struck it at the head, where it branched out into woody and briery ponds; and thence curved away, till, at the distance of three-quarters of a mile, it made its outlet into Port Royal River. The dogs had not long crept into its penetralia, before they gave forth their inspiring notes, and we were soon on the alert, lifting ourselves in our stirrups, to spy out, if it were possible, the object of pursuit. But the thicket spread around them with the density of a wall, and nothing could be seen! Again and again, they went circling around, close to where we stood; but it was as impracticable to approach as to see. Quicksand underneath, quagmire at the surface, briers above (wherever their places were not preoccupied by bay-trees, that, for want of elbow room, had grown up as straight as canes, and almost as close), this

10—C. S.

ground would have foiled the boldest moss trooper
that ever pricked his steed across the moors of Cum-
berland. At last the dogs came to a halt!—and we
knew by their quick, open note, that they had the
chase at bay. It was at this moment that Dash,
espying something in motion in the leafy top of a
bay-tree, cracked off his Joe Manton with such good
effect, that presently we heard a heavy body come
tumbling through the limbs until it splashed into
the water. Then came a stunning burst from the
hounds—a clash from the whole orchestra in full
chorus!—a growl from the assailed, with an occasional squeak on the part of the assailants, which
showed that the game was not all on one side. We
were compelled, all the while, to be delighted ear-
witnesses only of the strife, which resulted in the
victory of the hounds; and one of our drivers having
succeeded, by dint of creeping, dodging, clambering
and wading, in worming his way to the scene of
conflict, came forth with a fat, over-grown raccoon;
who thus paid forfeit with his life, for having
imprudently crossed the hounds, when intent on
higher game.

Strapping his prize across his shoulders, and
smacking his lips in advance, at the thought of the
high-flavored hams, into which he meant to convert his haunches, our driver pushed again into the
thicket with his dogs, while the horsemen kept the
open ground on the flank. And now we had nearly
reached the extremity of the gall, and began to fear

that we should start no other cat, when Rowser suddenly burst out into a fierce cry, as, emerging from the cover, he touched the open field. The hounds rush to the spot, second his alarm, and strike off at once for the margin near by. Hurra! they have struck a trail. Gather, huntsmen! Now we shall see sport! The ground was favorable for the sportsmen, for a road ran parallel with the direction of the cry, and thus the whole field got placed. and took a fair start with the dogs. "There they go! Look! for the hedge! Rowser leads—he leaps the hedge—ha! he has overrun the track. Black has caught it up—it is all right! There they go—look at them! —listen to them! Huntsmen, is it not charming? Does it not make your pulse quicken? Is there not a thrill of pleasure shooting through your frame? Can you tell your name? Have you a wife? a child? *Have you a neck?*" If you can, at such a moment, answer questions such as these, you do not feel your position and are but half a sportsman!

The run was an uncommon one for a cat, as it lay for a mile on end, through an open field. Forewarned of his danger, by the din which the dogs had made in pursuit of the raccoon, he had made this push, in order to get out of their reach. Vain effort!—the scent lies too strong—the nose of his pursuers is too keen! And now, the sight was exhilarating in the extreme. The pack ran in a cluster; the scent breast high; the whole field keeping close in their rear, and animating them by

their shouts. "Have a care! ride not too close! cross
not the track! fair play for the hounds, and they
will work it out. Now, rein in your horse along
with me. Do you note the *tone* of the cry? It is
not with such a tone they pursue a deer. I have
blown off my hounds from a chase, on no better
authority than the key on which they pitched their
cry. This cry is not prompted by the instinct of
hunger—it breathes hatred, antipathy! Look at
Wormwood there, the rascal!—how his hair bris-
tles on his back—what venom in his tones! and,
let me tell you (take care of that stump), I have
observed some packs, that run but upon two legs,
eager, like this, to rend and destroy, who betrayed,
by the tone of *their* cry, that their motive and their
cue to action, was just as hound-like! But see, they
push for the wood. He has tried a turn among the
saw palmettoes to perplex the scent. It won't do;
they trail him out through the open field to the river-
skirt! There we must have him!"

The ground on which the cat had sheltered himself, was a narrow thicket on the margin of the
marsh. Briers and saw palmettoes covering the
surface, made it very uncomfortable for the hounds
to pursue; while an almost unbroken line of pine,
oak, and bay-trees, intertwined with vines, made it
impracticable for horsemen. There were narrow
gaps, however, through which we expected to get
an occasional glimpse of him—perhaps a shot.
The hounds pressed eagerly on, through all this

tangle, to the extremity of the skirt; and when we momently expected they would drive him out into the open land, behold! they had lost the track! We looked up at the trees, to see whether he had secreted himself among their dense branches. We tried, first this path, and then that; we beat the back track: all in vain—hunter and hound stood at complete fault. It was hard to say whose disappointment was the greater. But what is Rowser after? See, he is running down the old field to the extreme end of the thicket, where a fence crosses from the wood. What does he there? Shade of Watts, Duncan and Hedge! can he syllogize? Hark! hark! he has struck the trail—listen to his joyous cry, "$\varepsilon v \rho \eta \kappa a$!" He sounds the alarm; how uproariously the whole pack second him. Sagacious animal, he has unmasked the stratagem of the cat— fairly countermined him!

While the hounds were running down the thicket, the cat, it would appear, unseen by hunter or hound, had executed a double, above their heads, by leaping from tree to tree, until, having threaded out the thicket, he had again ventured on terra firma, to gain the shelter in the wood. We had hardly plunged into the wood, to follow the direction taken by the hounds, when a shot from the old field in the rear told us that the cat had again doubled, to regain the thicket. A neighboring planter, who had been called out by the unusual din of our sport, had stumbled on him while executing his retreat, and saluted him with a load of bird shot. Two terriers, which had followed him into the field, now fifed in, to the louder clamor of the hounds; the pointers, obedient to evil example, were no longer content to leave the sport to the regular practitioners, but chimed in likewise with their sharp and shrill notes; and the uproar was delicious!

Look at Dash! he is pushing for the margin as fast as spur can drive him—he reins in his horse, and cracks away with duck-shot—"your distance is too great, that shot won't tell!" There is the cat, leaping from tree to tree, repeating the manœuvre by which he has already foiled us; but not unseen, as then. What! young cousin to a tiger, would you play the same game twice—on practised sportsmen, too? Dash starts to gain a nearer position. I reined up my horse, and took a hasty glance at the field. The movement of the cat was generally seen, and some were riding to get near, and some dismounting to get nearer; and many a gun was cocked, and many an eye fixed, and many a finger feeling for the trigger. This, then, is my chance, thought I; and off went one barrel, charged with duck-shot, apparently without effect; for the cat, with huge leaps, clambered up a tree; and now he had reached the very pinnacle, and as he gathered himself up to take a flying leap for a neighboring tree, I caught up my gun, and let slip at him in mid-flight. The arrowy posture in which he made his pitch, was suddenly changed, as the shot struck him to the heart; and doubling himself up, after one or two wild gyrations, into a heap, he fell dead, from a height of full fifty feet, into the very jaws of the dogs! It proved to be a female, smaller than the first cat, but beautifully spotted.

We stopped not long to admire, for the sun had now passed his meridian full two hours, and we had more than five miles to ride to our dinner. Behold us, then, in full gallop on our return. At three miles' distance from the town, we took up our first cat; and part of the field exchanged the saddle for a barouche, which here awaited us. And now, in high spirits, we dashed into town, our horns sounding a flourish as we approached—and our wild-cats, flanked by the raccoon, showing forth, somewhat ostentatiously, from the front of the barouche.

VENATOR.

A DAY AT CHEE-HA

The traveller in South Carolina, who passes along
the road between the Ashepoo and Combahee rivers
will be struck by the appearance of two lofty white
columns, rising among the pines that skirt the road.
They are the only survivors of eight, which supported, in times anterior to our revolutionary war,
a sylvan temple, erected by a gentleman,* who, to
the higher qualities of a devoted patriot, united the
taste and liberality of the sportsman. The spot was
admirably chosen, being on the brow of a piney
ridge, which slopes away at a long gun-shot's length
into a thick swamp; and many a deer has, we doubt
not, in times past, been shot from the temple when
it stood in its pride—as we ourselves have struck
them from its ruins. From this ruin, stretching
eastwardly some twelve or fourteen miles, is a neck
of land, known from the Indian name of the small
river that waters and almost bisects it, as Chee-ha—
or, as it is incorrectly written, Chy-haw! It is now
the best hunting-ground in Carolina—for which the
following reasons may be given. The lands are
distributed in large tracts; there are therefore few
proprietors. The rich land is confined to the belt
of the rivers, and there remains a wide expanse of

*Col. Barnard Elliott.

barrens, traversed by deep swamps, always difficult and sometimes impassable, in which the deer find a secure retreat.

At a small hunting-lodge located in this region, it has often been my good fortune to meet a select body of hunting friends, and enjoy in their company the pleasures of the chase.

I give you one of my "days"—not that the success was unusual, it was by no means so; but that it was somewhat more marked by incident than most of its fellows. We turned out, *after breakfast*, on a fine day in February, with a pack of twelve hounds, and two whippers in, or drivers, as we call them. The field consisted of one old shot besides myself, and two sportsmen who had not yet "fleshed their maiden swords." When we reached the ground, we had to experience the fate which all tardy sportsmen deserve, and must often undergo: the fresh print of dogs' feet, and the deep impression of horses' hoofs, showed us that another party had anticipated us in the drive, and that the game had been started and was off. Two expedients suggested themselves—we must either leave our ground, and in that case incur the risk of sharing the same fate in our next drive; or, we must beat up the ground now before us in a way which our predecessors in the field had probably neglected to do. We chose the latter part: and finding that the drive embraced two descriptions of ground—first, the main wood, which we inferred had already been taken, and next,

the briery thickets that skirted a contiguous old
field—into these thickets we pushed. Nor had we
entered far, before the long, deep, querulous note
of "Ruler," as he challenged on a trail, told us to
expect the game. A few minutes later, and the
whole pack announced the still more exciting fact—
"the game is up." The first move of the deer was
into a back-water, which he crossed, while the pack,
half swimming, half wading, came yelping at his
heels. He next dashed across an old field and made
for a thicket, which he entered; it was a piece of
briery and tangled ground, which the dogs could
not traverse without infinite toil. By these two
moves, he gained a great start of the hounds: if he
kept on, we were thrown out, and our dogs lost for
the day—if he doubled, and the nature of the ground
favored that supposition, there were two points
whereat he would be most likely to be intercepted.
I consulted the wind, and made my choice. I was
wrong. It proved to be a young deer, who did not
need the wind, and he made for the pass I had *not
selected*. The pack now turned; we found from their
cry, that the deer had doubled, and our hearts beat
high with expectation, as mounted on our respective
hunters, we stretched ourselves across the old field
which he must necessarily traverse, before he could
regain the shelter of the wood. And now I saw my
veteran comrade stretch his neck as if he spied
something in the thicket; then with a sudden fling
he brought his double barrel to his shoulder and

fired. His horse, admonished by the spur, then
fetched a caracole; from the new position, a new
glimpse of the deer is gained—and crack! goes the
second barrel. In a few moments, I saw one of our
recruits dismount and fire. Soon after, the deer
made his appearance and approached the second,
who descended from his horse and fired. The deer
kept on seemingly untouched, and had gained the
crown of the hill when his second barrel brought
him to the ground in sight of the whole field. We
all rode to the spot, to congratulate our novice on
his first exploit in sylvan warfare—when, as he
stooped to examine the direction of his shot, our
friend Loveleap slipped his knife into the throat of
the deer, and before his purpose could be guessed at,
bathed his face with the blood of his victim. (This,
you must know, *is hunter's law* with us, on the killing a first deer). As our young sportsman started
up from the ablution—his face glaring like an
Indian chief's in all the splendor of war-paint—
Robin the hunter touched his cap and thus accosted
him:

"Maussa Tickle, if you wash off dat blood dis day
—you neber hav luck again so long as you hunt."

"Wash it off!" cried we all, with one accord;
"who ever heard of such a folly. He can be no true
sportsman, who is ashamed of such a livery."

Thus beset, and moved thereunto, by other sage
advices showered upon him by his companions in
sport, he wore his bloody mask to the close of that

long day's sport, and sooth to say, returned to
receive the congratulations of his young and lovely
wife, his face still adorned with the stains of victory.
Whether he was received, as victors are wont to be,
returning from other fields of blood, is a point
whereon I shall refuse to satisfy the impertinent
curiosity of my dear reader; but I am bound, in
deference to historic truth, to add—that the claims
of our novice, to the merit and penalties of this day's
hunt, were equally incomplete, for it appeared on
after inspection, that Loveleap had given the mortal wound, and that Tickle had merely given the
"coup de grâce" to a deer, that, if unfired on, would
have fallen of itself, in a run of a hundred yards.
It must be believed, however, that we were quite too
generous to divulge this unpleasant discovery to our
novice, in the first pride of his triumph!

And now we tried other grounds, which our pre-
cursors in the field had already beaten; so that the
prime of the day was wasted before we made another
start. At last, in the afternoon, a splendid burst
from the whole pack made us aware that a second
deer had suddenly been roused. I was riding to
reach a pass (or *stand* as we term it), when I saw
a buck dashing along before the hounds at the top
of his speed; the distance was seventy-five yards—
but I reined in my horse and let slip at him. To
my surprise, he fell; but before I could reach the
spot, from which I was separated by a thick underwood, he had shuffled off and disappeared. The

hounds came roaring on, and showed me by their course that he had made for a marsh that lay hard by. For that we all pushed in hopes of anticipating him. He was before us, we saw him plunge into the canal, and mount the opposite bank, though evidently in distress and crippled in one of his hind legs. The dogs rush furiously on (the scent of blood in their nostrils), plunge into the canal, sweep over the bank, and soon pursuers and pursued are shut out from sight, as they wind among the thick covers that lie scattered over the face of the marsh.

"What use of horse now!" said Robin, as (sliding from his saddle where his horse instinctively made a dead halt at the edge of the impracticable Serbonian bog that lay before him) he began to climb a tree that overlooked the field of action—"what use of horse now?"

From this "vantage ground," however, he looked in vain to catch a glimpse of the deer. The eye of a lynx could not penetrate the thick mass of grass, that stretched upward six feet from the surface of the marsh. The cry of the hounds now grew faint from distance, and now again came swelling on the breeze; when suddenly our ears were saluted by a full burst from the whole pack, in that loud, open note, which tells a practised ear that the cry comes from the water.

"Zounds, Robin!" cried I, in the excitement of the moment, "they have him at bay there—there in the canal. Down from your perch, my lad, or they'll eat him, horns and all, before you reach him."

Robin apparently did not partake of this enthusiasm, for he maintained his perch on the tree, and coolly observed—"What use, massa? fore I git dere, dem dog polish ebery bone."

"You are afraid, you rascal! you have only to swim the canal and then"—

"Got maussa," said Robin, as he looked ruefully over the field of his proposed missionary labors; "if he be water, I swim 'em—if he be bog, I bog 'um—if he be brier, I kratch tru um—but who de debble, but otter, no so alligator, go tru all tree one time!"

The thought was just stealing its way into my mind, that under the excitement of my feelings, I was giving an order that I might have hesitated personally to execute, when the cry of the hounds, lately so clamorous, totally ceased. "There," cried I, in the disappointed tone of a sportsman who had lost a fine buck, "save your skin, you loitering rascal! You may sleep where you sit, for by this time they have eaten him sure enough." This conclusion was soon overset by the solitary cry of Ruler, which was now heard, half a mile to the left of the scene of the late uproar.

"Again! What is this? *It is* the cry of Ruler! ho! I understand it—the deer is not eaten, but has taken the canal—and the nose of that prince of hounds, has scented him down the running stream.

—Aye, aye, he makes for the wood—and now to cut him off." No sooner said than done. I gave the spur to my horse, and shot off accordingly; but not in time to prevent the success of the masterly manœuvre by which the buck, baffling his pursuers, was now seen straining every nerve to regain the shelter of the wood. I made a desperate effort to cut him off, but reached the wood only in time to note the direction he had taken. It was now sunset, and the white, outspread tail of the deer was my only guide in the pursuit, as he glided among the trees. "Now for it, Boxer—show your speed, my gallant nag." The horse, as if he entered fully into the purpose of his rider, stretched himself to the utmost, obedient to the slightest touch of the reins, as he threaded the intricacies of the forest; and was gaining rapidly on the deer, when plash! he came to a dead halt—his fore legs plunged in a quagmire, over which the buck with his split hoofs had bounded in security. What a baulk! "but here goes"—and the gun was brought instantly to the shoulder, and the left-hand barrel fired. The distance was eighty yards, and the shot ineffectual. Making a slight circuit to avoid the bog, I again push at the deer and again approach. "Ah, if I had but reserved the charge, I had so idly wasted!" But no matter, I must run him down—and gaining a position on his flank, I spurred my horse full upon his broad-side, to bear him to the ground. The noble animal (he *was* a noble animal, for he traced, with some baser admixture indeed, through Boxer, Medley, Gimcrack, to the Godolphin Arabian) refused to trample on his fellow quadruped; and, in spite of the goading spur, ranged up close along side of the buck, as if his only pride lay in surpassing him in speed. This brought me in close contact with the buck. Detaching my right foot from the stirrup, I struck the armed heel of my boot full against his head; he reeled from the blow and plunged into a neighboring thicket—too close for horse to enter. I fling myself from my horse, and pursue on foot—he gains on me: I dash down my now useless gun, and, freed from all encumbrance, press after the panting animal. A large, fallen oak lies across his path; he gathers himself up for the leap, and falls exhausted directly across it. Before he could recover his legs, and while he lay thus poised on the tree, I fling myself at full length upon the body of the struggling deer—my left hand clasps his neck, while my right detaches the knife; whose fatal blade, in another moment, is buried in his throat. There he lay in his blood, and I remained sole occupant of the field. I seize my horn, but am utterly breathless, and incapable of sounding it: I strive to shout, but my voice is extinct from fatigue and exhaustion. I retrace my steps, while the waning light yet sufficed to show me the track of the deer—recover my horse and gun, and return to the tree where my victim lay. But how apprise my comrades of my position? My last shot, however,

had not been unnoted—and soon their voices are
heard cheering on "Ruler," while far in advance of
the yet baffled pack, he follows unerringly on the
tracks of the deer. They came at last: but found
me still so exhausted from fatigue, that to wave my
bloody knife, and point to the victim where he lay at
my feet, were all the history I could give them of the
spirit-stirring incidents I have just recorded. Other
hunting matches have I been engaged in, wherein
double the number of deer have been killed; but
never have I engaged in one of deeper and more
absorbing interest than that which marked this
"day at Chee-ha."

VENATOR.

" I fling myself at full length upon the body of the struggling deer—my
left hand clasps his neck, while my right detaches the knife; whose fatal
blade, in another moment, is burried in his throat."

11—C. S.

ANOTHER DAY AT CHEE-HA

The sportsman, who gives a true description of his sports, *must be an egotist.* It is his *necessity.* The things which *he* has seen or done are precisely those which make the liveliest impression; and with none other, but such as are thus brightly enshrined in his memory, should he attempt the difficult task of interesting the careless or preoccupied. Let this be my apology for speaking of myself; and if in my narrations there is (as some friendly critic may suggest) a *want of repose,* it is as well for me candidly to confess that the *want* is intentional. I sin through design—and say, as Gilfert said, when notified of a drop stitch in the flesh-colored unmentionables of a celebrated danseuse pirouetting at the Bowery: "Hush, my friend, *dat is for effect.*" Could I rouse you an elephant, gentlemen critics, you should have a grave and stately march; I'd give you *repose* with a vengeance. But, for your lighter game, dash splash on, with whip and spur! *Celerity of movement* is the play—whether in the field or in the narrative!

It was a glorious winter's day—sharp but bracing. The sun looked forth with dazzling brightness, as he careered through a cloudless sky; and his rays came glancing back from many an ice-covered lagoon that lay scattered over the face of the ground.

The moan of an expiring northwester was faintly heard from the tops of the magnificent forest pines. Three sportsmen, while it was yet early, met at their trysting-place, to perpetrate a *raid* against the deer! They were no novices, those huntsmen—they had won trophies in many a sylvan war; and they now took the field "of malice prepense," with all the appliances of destruction at their beck; practised drivers and a pack, often proved, and now refreshed by three days' rest. Brief was their interchange of compliment; they felt that such a day was not to be trifled away in talk; and they hallooed their hounds impatiently into the drive—yet not as greenhorns would have done. "Keep clear of the swamps," was the order to the drivers—"leave the close covers— ride not where the ice crackles under the horse's hoof—but look closely into the sheltered knolls, where you will find the deer sunning themselves after the last night's frost." The effect of this order was soon evident; for in the second knoll entered by the hounds, a herd of deer were found thawing themselves in the first beams of the ascending sun. Ho! what a burst!—with what fury the hounds dash in among them! Now they sweep along the thickets that skirt the drive, and climb the summit of that elevated piney ridge—destined one day to become a summer settlement, and to bear the name of ——. But not unforeseen or unprovided for was the run which the deer had taken. Frisky Geordy was in their path, and crack went the sound of his gun, and loud and vaunting was the twang of his horn, that followed the explosion! And now the frozen earth reëchoed to the tramp of horses' hoofs, as the huntsmen hurried to the call, that proclaims that a deer has fallen. There was Geordy, his gun against a pine, his knee upon the still heaving flank of a *pricket buck*, his right hand clenched upon his dripping knife, his left flourishing a horn, which ever and anon was given to his mouth, and filled the air with its boastful notes.

"Holla, Geordy! you have got him fast, I see. Where are the dogs?"

"Gone," said Geordy.

"There's Ruler in the east—what's he after?"

"A deer," says Geordy.

"And Rouser to the south—what's he after?"

"Another deer," says Geordy.

"And Nimrod to the southwest—I need not ask what he's after, for he follows nothing but deer. Your second barrel snapt, of course?"

"I don't say that," says Geordy; "I had *wounded* the six last deer I'd fired at, so I thought I'd *kill* one to-day, and while I looked to see if that was really dead, the others slipt by me."

"Done like a sportsman, Geordy; one dead deer is worth a dozen crippled ones. I remember, once, your powder was too weak; and next, your shot were too small; and next, your aim was somewhat wild; and one went off bored of an ear, and another nicked of a tail. You are bound to set up an infirmary across the river, for the dismembered deer you have dispatched there! You have done well to *kill*—let it grow into a habit. Nimrod to the south-west, said you? That rascal is a born economist; and not a foot will he budge in pursuit of a *living deer*, after your horn has told him there is *venison* in the rear! Ruler will drive *his* deer across the river. Rouser to the marshes. Nimrod's quarry is the only one likely to halt and give us another chance."

And sure enough, there came Nimrod trotting back on his track—his nose cocked up in the air, as if to indorse and verify the inferences of his *ear*—his tail curled and standing out from his body, at an angle of 45°.

"This is the safe play—hang up the deer—sound your horn till the hounds come in from their several chases—and then for Nimrod's lead! to Chapman's bays, I think!—there are some sheltered nooks in which they will stop and bask, when they find themselves unpursued."

"I'll go in with the boys," says Loveleap, with an unconcerned air, but a sly twinkle of the eye, which did not escape his comrades.

"As you like—Geordy and I will mind the stands."

Some time was lost before the hounds could be drawn from their several chases, yet as emulation did not "prick them on," they came the sooner for being scattered. Loveleap heads the drivers—and it was just what we had anticipated, when, before a single dog had given tongue, we heard him fire, then came a burst, then a second barrel; but to our great surprise no horn announced the expected success. The report of that gun went unquestioned, in our sporting circle; it was in a manner axiomatic, in wood-craft mysteries, and passed current with all who heard it for thus much—"a deer is killed." Loveleap did an extraordinary thing that day—*he missed!* but the drivers could not understand, and the hounds would not believe it: so they rushed madly away in pursuit, as if it was not possible for the quarry long to escape.

"Push on," says Geordy, "they make for the river!" and away we went. We reined in for a minute at the ford; and finding that they had already outstripped us and were bearing down for Chapman's fort—a mile to the west of our position —we struck across for the marshes south of us, where we might, if he was a young deer, intercept him on his return to his accustomed haunts. If an old buck, we had no chance; *he* is sure to set a proper value on his life, and seldom stops until he has put a river between his pursuer and himself.

Taking advantage of a road that lay in our way, we soon cleared the woods, and entered an old field that skirted the marsh. It was a large waving plain of rank broom-grass, chequered here and there by strips of myrtle and marsh mallows.

"So far, Geordy," said I, "we have kept one track —now let us separate. The hounds are out of hearing, and we have little chance of any game but such as we may rouse without their help. How delightfully sheltered is this spot!—how completely is it shut in by that semi-circle of woods, from the sweep of the northwest winds! How genially the sun pours down upon it! Depend upon it, we shall find some luxurious rogues basking in this warm nook—for next to your Englishman, a deer is the greatest epicure alive! Now, then, by separate tracks, let us make across the old field—a blast of the horn will bring us together when we reach the marsh.

By separate tracks then we moved, and had not advanced two hundred yards, when crack! went Geordy's gun. I looked in the direction of the report—and his head only was visible above the sea of marsh mallows. The direction of his *face* I could see, and *that* was pointed toward me. Toward *me* then, thought I, runs the deer. I reined in my horse, and turned his head in that direction. It was such a thickly woven mass of mallows and myrtle—high as my shoulders as I sat in the saddle —that there was little hope of being able to see the game. I trusted to my ear to warn me of his approach, and soon heard the rustling of the leaves and the sharp quick leap, which mark the movement of a deer at speed. I saw him not, until he appeared directly under my horse's nose, in act to leap; he vaulted, and would have dropped upon my saddle, had he not seen the horse while yet poised in air,

and (by an effort like that of the tumbler who
throws a somerset) twisted himself suddenly to my
right. He grazed my knee in his descent; and as he
touched the earth I brought my gun down, pistol-
fashion, with a rapid twitch, and sent the whole
charge through his backbone. It was so instantaneous—so like a flash of lightning—that I could
scarcely credit it, when I saw the deer twirling and
turning over at my horse's heels. Dismounting to
secure him, it was some time before his muscular
action was sufficiently overcome to allow me to use
my knife. He struggled and kicked—I set down my
gun, the better to master him. In the midst of my
employment, crack went Geordy's second barrel,
nearer than the first—and *mind! mind!* followed the
discharge. Before I could drop my knife and gain
my feet, another deer was upon me! He followed
directly in the track of the former, and passed
between my horse and me, so near that I might have
bayoneted him? Where was my gun? lost in the
broom-grass! What a trial! I looked all around in
an instant, and spying it where it lay, caught it
eagerly up: the deer had disappeared! It flashed
across me, that underneath these myrtles, the limbs
excluded from the sun had decayed; and that in the
vistas thus formed, a glimpse of the deer might yet
be gained. In an instant I am on my knees, darting
the most anxious glances along the vista: the flash
of a tail is seen—I fire—a struggle is heard—I press
forward through the interlacing branches—and to

my joy and surprise, *another deer is mine!* Taking him by the legs, I drag him to the spot where the other lay. Then was it *my* turn to sound a "vaunty" peal! Geordy pealed in answer, and soon appeared, dragging a deer of his own (having missed one of those that I had killed). Three deer were started—they were all at our feet—and that *without the aid of a dog!* It was the work of five minutes! We piled them in a heap, covered them with branches and myrtle, and tasked our horns to the uttermost to recall the field. One by one the hounds came in—smelt at the myrtle bushes—seemed satisfied, though puzzled—wagged their tails—and coiling themselves each in his proper bed, lay down to sleep. Yet had any stranger approached that myrtle-covered heap, every back would have bristled, and a fierce cry of defiance would have broken forth from every tongue, then so mute.

At last came Loveleap, fagged, and somewhat fretted by his ill-success.

"I have been blowing till I've split my wind, and not a dog has come to my horn. How came you thrown out? and why have you kept such an incessant braying of horns? Why, how is this? the dogs are here?"

"Yes!—they have shown their sense in coming to us; there's been butchery hereabouts!"

"One of P——'s cattle killed by the runaways, I suppose."

"Will you lend us your boy to bring a cart?" said I.

"Certainly," says Loveleap; "it will make such a feast for the dogs; but where is the cow?"

"*Here!*" says Geordy, kicking off the myrtle screen, and revealing to the sight of his astonished comrade, *our three layers of venison!* Oh, you should have seen Loveleap's face!

The cart is brought, and our four deer are soon on their way home. Do you think we accompanied them? No! We were so merciless as to meditate still further havoc. The day was so little spent— and as our hands were in, and there was just in the next drive, an overgrown old buck, who had often had the insolence to baffle us,—no! we must take a drive for him! Again the hounds are thrown into cover, headed by our remaining driver; but in the special object of our move we failed—the buck had decamped. Still, *the fortune of the day* attended us; and an inquisitive old turkey gobbler, having ventured to peep at Geordy where he lay in ambush, was sprawled by a shot from his gun, and was soon seen dangling from his saddle-bow.

This closed our hunt. And now that we have a moment's breathing time, tell me, brother sportsmen! who may chance to read this veritable history —has it ever been your fortune, in a single day's hunt, and as the *spoils* of two gunners only, to bring home four deer and a wild turkey? Ye gastronomes! who relish the proceeds of a hunt better than its toils and perils—a glance at that larder, if you please! Look at that fine bird—so carefully hung up by the neck; his spurs are an inch and a half in length, his beard eight inches; what an ample chest! what glossy plumage!—his weight is twenty-five pounds! And see that brave array of haunches!— *that* is of a buck of two years—juicy, tender, but not fat—capital for steaks! But your eye finds something yet more attractive—the *saddle* of a four-year old doe, kidney covered, as you see; a morsel more savoury smokes not upon a monarch's board. How pleasant to eat! Shall I say it?—how much pleasanter to give away! Ah, how such things do win their way to *hearts*—men's, and *women's* too! My young sporting friends, a word in your ear: the worst use you can make of your game, is to eat it yourselves.

Ye city sportsmen! (we mean, par excellence, the sportsmen of the *Commercial Emporium*,) who, with abundant pains and trouble, and with note of fearful preparation, marshal your forces for a week's campaign among the plains of Long Island, or the barrens of Jersey—and in reward of your toil, bag one brace of grouse, or enjoy a *glorious snap* at some straggling deer, that escapes, *of course*, to tempt another party to your hopes and disappointments!— ye city sportsmen! who go so far, and get so little for your pains—what think ye of the execution done on this day, in a chase which cost us no extraordinary trouble, and never took us five miles from our winter homes? Or, ye enthusiasts in sport! who import from our shores the game, your own inhospitable winters deny to your wishes—whose *purchased* partridges leave their travelling coops, to hibernate in the warm attic of a Broadway palace— thence to be transferred in the spring to the *pro- tected* covers of Long Island—there to pair and rear broods, to be bagged in September, by the same paternal hand that imported and domesticated the parent stock! what think ye of sport like this? Ours was no *preserve* shooting! We were not popping over our own nurselings? They were wild deer, of the wild woods, that we slew, this day at Chee-Ha! Ye are of the right metal, we know, and it would please us to see you some day among us—and mark the throb of a new delight springing in your bosoms, as you sweep along with the rush of the hounds, and fling the cares of life far, far behind you.

VENATOR.

A BUSINESS DAY AT CHEE-HA

A FIG for the sportsman, who will only converse with you in the "King Cambyses vein!"—who is dumb, unless he boast of some magnificent sport, or some unequalled exploit! I have already told you, gentle reader, somewhat of my successes; shall I misjudge you, if I suppose that the recital of an occasional failure may prove almost as grateful?

It was the end of October. The first light frosts had fallen. The demons of pestilence, that for six months had rioted undisturbed in the dank vapors of our campagna; nipped by the northern blasts, now flapped their wings in dismay, and boomed off for the congenial fens of the remoter South. The planters who had intrenched themselves, all the while, in towns and villages against the assaults of their invisible but deadly foe, now rushed joyfully forth (like men from a beleaguered city on the withdrawal of the enemy) to revisit their forsaken plantations. I, among the rest, was preparing for my first visit to Chee-Ha. It was a visit of inspection—of *business*—to see how my interest had fared during the long summer's absence. Yet, somehow or other, Robin the huntsman was the servant chosen to attend me, and my hunting pony was the horse he was to mount; and my gun and horn were thrown into the gig, as if a necessary part of my travelling equipment; and Rowser, Black and Nimrod, with an instinctive perception that *their* day of importance was come, crouched whimpering at my feet, then trotted off in company as if they had been regularly summoned; so that it was apparent that if *a hunt* was not exactly the direct object of my visit, it might readily become a collateral one.

The journey is made, and the night passed in that venerable and hospitable mansion, to which Loveleap, from a different quarter, but with purposes similar to my own, had but just repaired. The morning dawned, and the first beams of the sun found us dressed, walking the piazza and rejoicing in the promise of a glorious day. The air was cold; the vapors that hovered about the river, condenced by the night's cold, and lifted by the rays of the ascending sun, were looped up in the horizon like a broad curtain, which left the roots and tops of the trees distinctly visible, while the intermediate parts were still shrouded in its dense folds.

"A charming day," said Loveleap, stretching his neck impatiently beyond the railing to observe the course of some thin strata of clouds that moved slowly in the higher region of the atmosphere. "There will be no wind—so moist, too; the scent will lie famously."

"Too true," said I, "but you know I come on business; 'business before pleasure,' that's my motto."

"But will your business hold you all day? Could you not dispatch it, and after, take a hunt?"

"Possibly," said I.

"Then I will call my boy," said Loveleap, and seizing his horn, gave a loud blast which brought not his boy only, but the whole eager pack of expecting hounds upon us in a moment, wagging their tails, whining with anticipated pleasure and casting their noses up into the air, as if they already caught the scent of the out-lying deer! The appeal was irresistible.

"Tempt me no more, Loveleap; I will swallow a hasty breakfast, and gallop over to my plantation. Give me three hours for business—the rest of the day shall be yours!"

The breakfast is ended, the horse mounted.—"In three hours I shall expect you," said I at parting, and away I go at a hand gallop. The road lay through my corn fields; but the grain had been gathered. "Why should I pause to observe it narrowly? Some better drainage is wanted, I can see at a glance; but that is past and incurable; before another crop all that shall be remedied; and there are my peas ungathered—their bearing is truly abundant; but what is this? a deer's track! two of them, by Jove!—not two nights since have they cropped these leaves, as I know by the freshness of the tooth-print! My dainty, sleek-skinned marauders, you shall account to me for this! And there is my cotton-field on the hill to the right: it lies out of my way, a distant coup d'œil must serve me now, some other time I shall examine it closely." Oh! it is wonderful how we stride over the field of business, when we have hitched to the fence beyond, some favorite hobby which we are impatient to mount and ride!

And now the noisy chirping of a thousand blackbirds, clustered on a neighboring tree; and the merry clatter of the flail rebounding from the barn-yard floor, announced the approach to the settlement. The overseer crawled forth to greet me, pale and still feeble from the inflictions of the autumnal scourge; and yet this man had done no bodily labor—he had not toiled under our burning skies; but rode habitually to the fields to superintend the work of the blacks, and was sheltered from sun and rain by an umbrella!—and is it *this* region which the philanthropic abolitionist would people with white laborers? The Asiatic cholera would not be more sweeping in its desolation, more unsparing or more fatal than this pestilent malaria. Is not the scheme of superseding slave labor in such a region by free white labor, as insane and atrocious as that of Lequinio, who proposed to perpetuate republican principles by exterminating all of the human family who were old enough to have imbibed the taint of monarchy? *His* benevolence would reach but one generation of men, the wider philanthropy of the abolitionist would reach even to extermination.

I enter the barn-yard; the driver doffs his hat and draws a long scrape of the right foot by way of welcome; and the glossy-backed operatives hedge

me about with a circle of flail sticks, by way of
salute. What greasy-looking rogues! What a
contrast to the bloodless, fever-stricken being who
was placed there to superintend their labors! The
dank vapors of the swamps, so baneful to him—
had they served to nourish *their* grosser bodies?
Had they fattened on the mere aroma of the rice,
like the poor Parisian on the fumes of the pastrycook
shop? It was not that they had fed on it, surely,
for there stood their own ricks unthreshed. Could
they have stolen it? "The theft of a slave is no
offence against society;" says a high legal authority;
and these slaves had possibly acted on the principle,
and had not been looked to over closely in so doing;
for there is a precept better known to the southern
planter than to the philanthropist who condemns
him: "Muzzle not the ox that treadeth out the
corn."

I mount the steps of the winnowing house; it had
a twofold advantage; it enabled me to glance at once
over the whole extent of the rice-fields, and to count
the ricks of rice in the barn-yard. I will not detain
you, gentle reader, by describing the rich appearance
of the rice fields as viewed from that eminence; the
deep, golden hues of the newly-reaped stubble,
relieved by the fresh green of the leaves shooting out
from the roots to bourgeon forth (if the season
allowed it) into a second harvest. Nor will I fatigue
you by recalling the pleasant thoughts that possess
the planter's mind, when, looking down on those

12—C. S.

capacious ricks, he dwells on the amount of sus-
tenance to man and other animals which they provide, or calculates the ample profits to himself. You,
like myself, may be anxious for a hunt, and I shall
not long detain you.

"Have you threshed out a rick?"

"Yes, sir," says the driver.

"What was the yield to the acre?"

"Sixty bushels, sir."

"Was it your best rick?"

"N—o, sir."

"Mixed you any of the straw rice with this rick?"

"Y—es, sir, a lettle; but you kin see, maussa!"
and the driver brought me a sheaf from a rick hard
by—thick, full-grained, heavy; a magnificent sample (if true sample it was) of the crop which was
to reward my expectation. Alas, Venator! thou
knewest not that the rick was *plated*, or rather
gilt; and that while the outward and tangible sheaf
was of such satisfactory quality, the light, and the
mow-burnt, and the bird-pecked was safely bestowed,
far from the reach of inquisitive eyes, in the very
centre of those proud looking ricks! How like a
honeymoon in the planter's life are the first brief
visits of the fall, to the long deserted plantations!
All then is bright and full of glorious promise; but
winter comes, and at its close—the hour of disen-
chantment!

On descending from the winnowing house a long,
slab-sided fellow stalks up to me—

"Maussa, cum tell you, sir, me clote an't nuff."

"Did you not get your six yards?"

"Ees, sir."

"That was enough."

"Ees, sir; but Anty Phillis cut me long tail blue so long, ee only lef wun leg to me britches."

"Can't help it."

"Ki, maussa! me guine stan een ban-yard widout no britches!"

"Maussa!" said a strapping young jade, advancing with a shoe in her hand, "me shoo no fit."

"Can't help that; take it to the overseer."

"Enty I carry um ready, an' I say obshaa, maussa no low dis; an he cuss at you!"

"Curse?"

"Ees, maussa, obshaa, him say, cause me gon cut me medjure haf inch too short:—him no care a dam! Enty dat de cuss?"

"Maussa! maussa!" said several voices at once, offering, to my unwilling ear, petitions equally important and edifying with the foregoing; but at that moment a shrill whistle, rather than a blast from the horn of Loveleap (this was his private signal), warned me of his approach, and I hastily dismissed this high court of appeals, with the remark: "Another time; when you have found out your grievances, I will find time to attend to them. I must now go to visit the sick;" and off I galloped for the negro quarters. Their houses were arranged in a double row; and in the midst sat a grey haired mauma, surrounded by a troop of little negroes, over whom she exercised plenary authority. The sick were then visited, examined and prescribed for. Fortunately, there were no serious cases, and I was preparing to depart, when the plantation nurse, who had been whiling away the tedium of her unoccupied hours in a sound day sleep, hobbled forth to meet me.

"Huddee, maussa!—how you do?"

"Well."

"How missis do?"

"Well."

"An' all de fambly?"

"Well—all well."

"Bress de Lord! An' young missis, too?"

"I've told you she was well."

"An' me leetle young missis, too, and young mass Pincher?" continued the interminable interrogator, who, in spite of all impediment, was determined to fire off her whole volley of questions.

"Have you no sick but those I have visited in yonder house?"

"Ees, sir; Cudjo got a bad toot."

"Out with it."

"And Diana, too; him got twins!"

"Nurse them!"

"Only him not got baby clothes for *two!*"

"That's her fault; why did she not give me notice?"

"Eh! eh! maussa too komkil! How now 'bout

wood?—cause Hacklus back so stiff, him no sarbis to me—can't stoop for pick up stick, for warm de hous; so please let Uncle Jupter help, or de little niggers will ketch a perish!"

"That you might sleep all day!"

"Ki, ole maussa! When young Mass Pincher cummin een place? I yerre ee ride hoss fur kill! ole maussa!"

"Not a word more!" cried I, flinging myself into the saddle with rather more effort than was needful; and twisting round my gun between my finger and thumb, as if it was as light as a riding-whip. " '*Old Maussa!*' you shall not say *that*. No," said I, as some unpleasant memories flashed across my mind; "not for two years to come!"

"Tink of dat now!" said the disappointed nurse, as she hobbled back to her bed, to sleep out the remnant of her nap; "he hair 'gin to turn grey, and he bex caus I call um ole!"

"Well, Loveleap," said I as he now advanced, followed by drivers and hounds, "I am at your service. Have my three hours expired?"

"Only two," said Loveleap; "but knowing your talent for dispatch of business, I borrowed one, and am here."

We struck for the woods across a back-water dam. The horse-path cut the preceding year was over-hung with twigs of the summer growth; and every-thing looked as still and unfrequented, as the lover of nature or the lover of sport could desire. The

trout sprang from beneath the willow, as the little
insects, scared by our approach, or shaken from
the interlacing branches, fell into the smooth lake
below.   The summer duck rose with a shrill cry,
from his woody screen; and the teal, that with bills
beneath their wings, were quietly reposing and
digesting their last night's gleanings from the rice-
fields, shot off on whistling wing to seek some less
disturbed retreat. The woods now broke upon us in
all their autumnal glory. The sweet gum, the maple,
and the hickory spread their branches as a canopy
above our heads; and the bright hues of their red
or yellow foliage, contrasted pleasingly with the
sombre verdure of the pine. Some lingering flowers,
too, were there; and the vanilla, touched by the
frosts, filled the forest with a fragrance exceeding
even the perfumes of spring.   And then those
coverts; so solitary, so undisturbed! whose repose
had not been startled for months, by the baying of a
hound, or the echoes of the huntsman's horn! My
heart bounded within me, as we cast off the pack,
and rode rapidly forward to guard the passes of the
drive.

It was *Wright's Bay*, and the dogs had scarcely
entered, when they roused a deer, and went roaring
on in pursuit through the centre of the drive; while
we dashed on at full speed along a foot-path that
incircled it. We were too late; the deer had escaped
by *Green Pond!*

"Push on, Tippoo," said Loveleap to his roan, "we'll catch him yet at *Chapman's Bay!*"

Too late again! away went the deer for the river, and when our panting steeds drew up at the brink, the deer had already crossed, and the leading dogs were howling along the bank, and asking, as far as their brute action could ask it—our leave to follow.

"Too fast for us this time," said Loveleap, "we'll try it again."

At slower pace than we had come, we retraced our steps, and cast off the dogs a second time into the same drive. The same ill-success attended us: again we started—again the deer got ahead of us, and again we toiled in an unprofitable chase, until we again found ourselves pell mell with the hounds at Chapman's fort, the deer having again crossed the river!

"I'll tell you what, Loveleap," said I, "this is sorry sport to me! I have little of the Osbaldistone in me, and relish not these hard rides against time; the deer, it seems, are grown so timid from the 'corruptions of a long peace,' that they trust neither to their legs nor wind; but push, on the first alarm from the dogs, directly for the river. Ride back, if it pleases you; for myself I decline a third heat, and shall rub down and cool off here."

The indefatigable Loveleap turned back to renew the hunt, while I remained to intercept the deer, if, on another start, he should repeat the same run.

The period of his absence seemed long. I dismounted; and throwing the reins over my horse's head, left him to graze at will, while I seated myself on the small mound of earth which dignifies this spot with the name of *Fort:* and as the dark waters of the Ashepoo glided noiselesly by, flinging here and there a bubble to the surface, which broke or disappeared to give place to other bubbles; and as the leaves, fanned by a gentle southern air, fell rustling from the surrounding trees to mingle with and be lost in the earth that received them, I mused, and bethought me that they were but too apt emblems of human fortunes, and human life! Where were the original lords of this soil, whose dark forms glided, in by-gone days, through these forests; intent, like ourselves, on the pleasures of the chase? Gone like those bubbles! scattered like the leaves of a former season by the blast of the whirlwind, or buried (as those now falling about me were soon to be) undistinguished beneath the soil! their musical dialect every day upon our tongues, and they—forgotten as though they had never been! And where were they who dispossessed them? the early white colonists?—gone like themselves! The spreading oaks hard by, marked their traditionary graves; but their histories, their very names, already indistinct from time, are fading day by day from human memory! Shall we, too, pass away and be forgotten? must the like oblivion rest on us, and on the race to which we belong? What unthought-of page,

in the unsearchable book of futurity, might yet be
ours! I was roused from these reveries by a sound
like that of a distant gun; it was very indistinct;
it might be the stroke of the woodman's axe—or
the crash of a falling tree; it roused me, however,
and, mounting my horse, I rode a short distance to
the east of my late position, and stood in the gorge
of a small ravine, open in front, whence I com-
manded the bluff on the left and the marsh on my
right.   I might have relapsed into my former
musing, but for a restless motion of my horse's ears,
which riveted my attention. Could he hear what
was inaudible to me? I listened—and it did seem to
me that I heard the cry of hounds. Was it fancy?
No!—it is too distinct for that!—and hark! they
approach. The distinguishing notes of the leading
hounds could now be heard; but they dropped in at
intervals, as if they were running at wide distances
in a weary chase. Aye, they near me!—and, by the
sound, are bearing down directly for this spot! and
my pulse beat high with expectation, as settling
myself in my saddle, I glanced my eye over lock and
barrel to see that all was right. The pack were still
nearly a mile distant, when a deer sprang suddenly
from the thicket into the ravine before me and stood.
It was a peg-horned buck; he turned his head back,
and pricked his delicate ears in the direction of the
cry; then, after a moment's pause, as if to determine
his course, he leaped forward to gain the river.
There was an air of security about him, amounting

almost to playfulness, and he threw up his hind legs with a sort of gambolling motion, as much as to say to his pursuers: "*That* for you, you wide-mouth'd curs! your throats are good, but as for your legs—*that* for you; and when you get thus far—a cool swim to you across the Ashepoo!"

I sat motionless on my horse until he had approached within fifty yards, when, snatching up my gun, I fired and he fell. Dismounting and laying down my gun, I advanced to secure him, when, suddenly regaining his legs, he slipped through my fingers, and scrambling under the limbs of a low-spreading oak, floundered off into a thicket and was lost to view. Aware that his aim would be the river, I rode quickly back to the bluff, and shouted at the top of my voice. The noise of my gun and my shouts now reached the pack, reviving their failing strength, and they bore down toward me with renewed speed—still I rode and shouted, in order to turn back the deer, and hoping that they might intercept him on their advance. The leading dogs now reached the spot where the deer had fallen; there was his blood sprinkled over leaf and sod—but where was the deer? The laggards of the pack, the cold of nose but slow of foot, now dropped in; but they all stood at complete fault! Nimrod alone (he was from a cross with the West India blood-hound), traced him out on his back track, as making a circuit to my left, he was working his way to the river. I heard his cry of alarm, and galloping in the direction, saw him seize the deer and hold him fast, when he was but thirty yards distant from the river. The other hounds were not up; and a second time I dismounted to lay hold of him. Before I touched the ground, he broke away from the dog and pushed for the river. I raised my gun, but the dog was so close at his heels that I could not fire without killing both. As he mounted the parapet, an interval of a few feet was gained; I fired, and the deer rolled over the mound *into the river!* At this moment a horseman arrived. It was Robin.

"Lay hold of his horns, Robin—they are within reach of the shore." Robin stooped, but the deer, not quite dead, gave a kick which propelled him a yard from the shore. "Here is a rail, pass it over him and draw him to you." The rail broke short in his hand, and the dogs, now drawn to the spot by the uproar, plunged in, seized the deer by the ears, and instead of landing him, dragged him further and further into the river.

"In with you, Robin," said I, "or he's lost. There's not an instant to spare; in with you!"

"My Got, Maussa! dem dog tek me for deer and drown me."

"Drown *you*, you prince of fools!—they know an ass from a deer."

"Anty de ribber deep, maussa?"

"Deep!—was ever man cursed with so cowardly a driver? I'll in myself, and bring him ashore;" and I kicked off my boots, unbuckled my stock, stripped off my coat, and was preparing for the last sacrifice* to the Graces, when Loveleap, who had ridden up during the turmoil, casting a queerish look at me, asked: "Do you mean to swim after it?"

"I do," said I.

"You are hot," said Loveleap.

"Hot!—would it not fever a saint, to have that fellow fail at this pinch, who never failed before?—ask if the river's deep, as if it mattered a sixpence whether it was one fathom or a hundred! Have I not trained him until he is amphibious, and does not know the difference between land and water?"

"I mean you are heated—too much so to go in until you are cooler. I have not ridden hard, nor scuffled with the deer, as you seem to have done; I am a better swimmer, too, and see—that eddy has swept the deer further into the stream."

With this, he began to undress; and I, thinking it idle that two should take the plunge, when one would suffice to land the prize, began to replace my clothes as he divested himself of his; and indeed, the exposure of my person, heated by the struggle, to the cold air from the river, already made me shiver! When I was completely dressed, Loveleap still applied himself to the task of undressing, but more deliberately, it seemed to me, than before. At last the work was ended, and his manly form, untrammelled by dress, stood prominently forth on

*I differ from Coleman, who uses the expression: "Sacrificing to the Graces by putting *on* his clothes," etc.

the river's brink, like the statue of one of the Athletæ of ancient Greece! The Naiads of the Ashepoo blushed deep, and hid their faces within her sedgy banks, as the unwonted image stood mirrored in her dark stream! Thus stood Leander in act to leap, when the love lamp in the distant tower, taught him to contemn the cold waters of the Hellespont: and thus stood Loveleap; but no Hero beckoned *him*, from beyond the cold flood! He stood, but leaped not; and casting a rueful look at the deer, now receding in the distance:

"That cursed eddy," said he, "has twirled him into the middle of the stream; and see—he has been sucked into the strength of the tide. Do you think there is no danger?"

"If *you* think there is," said I, after a pause, "it is enough: there is no more to be said—dress yourself—the deer is lost." Then turning toward the unconscious deer, whose head and peg horns were alone visible, as it floated rapidly up the stream, I vented my disappointment in this apostrophe: "Go, thou fool! no better than Napoleon, hast thou known the fitting time to die! *The devil* take thee, for thou hast needlessly kicked and thrust thyself beyond the reach of *a blessing!*" and with this grotesque comparison and forced pun, which, strange to say, seemed to blunt the edge of my vexation, I set spurs to my horse, and soon left behind me the scene of so many unpleasant memories.

Loveleap overtook me, when, my disappointment having expended itself a little, my pace had proportionably slackened.

"I had two chances to have blown off his head," said I, "before he gained the river, and I stupidly let them slip: and why? because I have a foolish pride in letting each barrel tell for a deer! I am vexed that he is lost; I had sooner have lost the finest bullock in my herd."

"Console yourself," said Loveleap, "we'll talk about it over a venison steak! Did you hear a gun?"

"I think I did," said I.

"A fine doe is waiting for us a mile ahead," said Loveleap.

"And that made you so confoundedly cool at the river side," said I.

"There were two started," said he, "the doe I shot, and the *peg horned* buck"——

"Is now floating up Ashepoo River," interrupted I, "his horn in the throat of the ravenous alligator that makes his supper of him!"

As I have occasionally consoled a brother sportsman for disappointments in the field, by reciting the mischance of this day, I have sometimes caught Loveleap slily tipping the wink to his neighbor, as much as to say: "I hummed him; my stripping was all a feint; meant to prevent his swimming Ashepoo River after a buck." It may be so; but if true, it shows that Loveleap has mistaken his vocation, and done wrong to devote his talents to wood-craft. He must equal old Perigord himself in diplomacy, for never man seemed more in earnest, or had more credit for being so.

VENATOR.

THE LAST DAY AT CHEE-HA

THE day was fine, and many a familiar face was noted at the gathering place. There was G——, of Port Royal, with his huntsman Dick, and his famous pack, that, sweeping like a whirlwind over the land, dashed across an ordinary river as if they scarcely counted it an impediment; nor checked their career, when their mettle was fairly roused, for anything short of an arm of the sea. He was mounted on his gallant roan; his person, youthful and erect, though the frosts had prematurely settled on his head—possibly from reflecting too bitterly on the perverseness of man—possibly from the toil of circumventing and sacrificing whole hecatombs of deer! Then came E. R——, of Beaufort. He had not laid aside his spectacles; but they no longer poured over the decisions of the Courts, nor glanced at the fees of clients, but rested unprofitably upon two polished barrels, which, yet, were pointed at nothing. He had his labor for his pains; yet he counted all labor as productive, and was content! Then came C——, of Bray's Island with "Big Thunder" sleeping on his thigh. It was anomalous thunder: it uttered no sound that day. Then came G. P. E——, of Smilie's. He made no puns, but wore a serious visage; meditating, perhaps, how he might provide new subjects for his infirmary!

Then came T. R. S——, of the "Bluff," (the Love-leap of our former histories) a sportsman accomplished in all the mysteries of wood-craft—yet not so resolved in sport as to swim a river after a buck. Then came T. R. S. E——, of "Balls"—at that time a stripling, yet willing, like David, to encounter Goliah himself, if he came in the shape of a buck or devil-fish! And, lastly, came myself—sometime "Piscator," but now "Venator," if your courtesy will allow him the designation. Three drivers, and upward of twenty hounds, completed the equipment for the hunt.

We assembled at "Social Hall;" and sending the drivers and hounds to enter the wood from the direction of "Smilie's," proceeded to occupy all the prominent passes of the "White Oak," stretching along, at intervals, from the flood-gate dam to "Sandy Run." My own stand was taken at the head of a long pond, or chain of ponds, which, approaching closely to the "White Oak," stretched away toward the southeast, until it found its outlet in Wright's Bay. I stood at the head of this pond on a knoll, that, piercing the swamp to the distance of one hundred and fifty yards, was flanked on either side by deep morasses, affording very thick cover. Standing among some dwarf trees that crowned the summit of this knoll, and which served as a partial screen, with my bridle reins thrown carelessly over my arm, I was listening to the cry of the hounds, as, at great distance, and at slow intervals, they challenged on a trail, when I caught a glimpse of a large dark object moving on my right; a second object was perceived, but still indistinct, and covered by the thicket. Presently a third and fourth were seen, and as they emerged from the dense cover, I perceived, to my great surprise, that they were *bears*. They were crossing the foot of the knoll on which I stood, from the right to the left. I leaped into the saddle, and as the ground in front was favorable to a horse, dashed at them to cut them off, if possible, before they had gained the cover on the left. I had not run more than half my career, when I reined in my horse; for I perceived that two of the bears had changed their course, and were coming toward me. Their object, I presume, was not *attack*, but *escape* from the hounds, whose distant baying they had heard. They ran straight for me, however, until they had approached within twenty yards; when the leading bear, a large one, stopped and looked me full in the face. A yearling bear followed, and, as if prompted by curiosity, reared himself on his hind legs and looked inquisitively over the shoulder of the leader. I seized the moment when their heads were thus brought in line, and almost in contact, and drew aim directly between the eyes of the larger bear. It occurred to me, at the instant, that my left-hand barrel was charged with shot of unusually large size, and I accordingly touched the left-hand trigger. Instantly the foremost bear disappeared, and the second,

uttering a cry of distress, rolled over among the
bushes, so as to assure me of its being seriously hurt;
but the glimpse I had of him was so imperfect, that
I did not fire my second barrel. Riding to the spot,
imagine my surprise at seeing the large bear motionless, and in the same upright posture which he
maintained before I fired; his head, only, had sunk
upon his knees! *He was stone dead!*—two shot had
pierced his brain. His death, apparently, had been
instantaneous—and the slight support of a fallen
tree, had enabled him to retain a posture by which he
yet simulated life! In searching for his wounded
companion, I was guided to the edge of the morass
by the torn earth and trampled grass; but there lost
all trace of him in the tangled underwood. Diverging
a little to the right, and following a faintly traced
path that penetrated the thicket, I again came upon
a trail. Evidently there were several that had taken
this direction: here was the foot-print, freshly
stamped in the muddy soil—here were the logs
which they had leaped, on their retreat, yet dripping
with the water splashed on them; but the bears had
passed onward, and the ground became more and
more difficult, until it prevented all further advance.

I was now in the heart of the swamp, and I
sounded my horn to call around me the hunters and
hounds, the first for consultation, the second for pursuit. No horn replied! I shouted—no answer! I
listened—and began to understand why my signals
were unnoticed. The hounds had roused a deer, and

were bearing down toward my left; and none of
the field were willing, by leaving their stands, or
answering a blast whose import they could not
understand, to forfeit their own chance of sport.
Nearer and nearer comes the cry—they are skirting
the thicket, and are driving directly for my stand!

"Well! let them come! I have one barrel yet in
reserve," and with this reflection, I make the best
of my way back to the position I had just occupied!
The chase turned to the left; presently a shot is
fired in that direction, but no horn sounds the signal
of success! "Ho! the dogs are gaining the pine
ridge in the rear, and may soon be lost—that must
not be"—and I dash away at full speed to intercept
them. It was no easy task to beat them off, heated
as they were in the chase, and stimulated by the
report of the gun. I rode across their track, and
shouted, and blew my horn; but all in vain—when
the drivers came up opportunely to my assistance!
By dint of chiding, and smacking of whips, they at
last succeeded in drawing off the hounds, that were
almost frantic with eagerness to pursue the deer!
The horns then sound a call, and the hunters come
dropping in.

"Why have you stopped the dogs?" said the
Laird, with something of brusquerie in his manner.

"Because they are out of the drive; and, if not
stopped, may be lost for the day."

"But I have shot a buck," said he.

"Where is he?"

"Gone on," said he; "but I'm sure they'll catch him in short order."

"So very sure!—found blood then?"

"No."

"How far off was he when you fired?"

"Oh, for that matter, he was jumping over me!"

"Then he carries shot bravely," said I; "but before we follow this buck—who, by your showing, cannot possibly go far—there is other business for the hounds: a nobler quarry is before us!—I have shot a bear!"

"A bear!" cried the hunters in astonishment. "You joke!—we never saw one in these woods!"

"True, nevertheless! Ride up with the hounds, and it will be hard but I will show you blood!"

And away we went at a rattling pace for the scene of action: some faces expressing confidence, and some mistrust! As we neared the spot:

"No joke, by gracious!" cried G—— (his piety forbidding any stronger exclamation). "Look at the dogs!—how the hair is bristling upon their backs; they smell the bear at this moment!"

And so, indeed, they did; for there he stood before them!—not fallen, but crouching, as if prepared to spring—yet, as we have said, *stone dead!*

It was pleasant to witness the surprise, and to receive the congratulations of my sporting friends, as they crowded around the bear—the horses showing uneasiness, however, and the dogs mistrust, amounting almost to terror!

While the drivers were encouraging the hounds to approach and familiarize themselves with the scent of the bear—which they were baying at a distance, as if they feared his quietude might be counterfeit—I dismounted and reloaded my left-hand barrel.

"And now, my friends," said I, on remounting, "We have glorious sport ahead!—a wounded bear is within fifty yards of us."

"Now we know you joke," said they in a breath; "you fired but one barrel!"

"But that," said I, "had bullets for two. I have shot another, as sure as a gun!—but *that* (glancing at him of the buck) is not always the highest assurrance! look here, at these bushes, torn up by his struggles—and this blood! He made his way into that thicket, and *there* we'll find him! Let us surround it—set on the dogs, and then hurra! for the quickest shot and the surest marksman!—only take care, as we stand so close, that we do not shoot each other!"

The hounds were now brought to the trail, while we shout and clap our hands in encouragement. But they were panic stricken, and would not budge a foot in advance of the drivers.

"Let us ride in," said Loveleap!

"Done," said I; and we placed ourselves, with G—— and C——, in the first line, while the other hunters, moving on the flanks, were in position to give their fire if he broke out.

"Here he is!" said C——, before we had advanced twenty yards into the thicket.

"Where?"

"Before me. I cannot see him, but my horse does, for he snorts and refuses to advance!"

We close our ranks, with finger on trigger, and hearts beating with expectation; but there was no room for chase, or fight—*the bear lay dead before us!* A grand hurra burst from us!—a grand flourish of horns!—and my hunting-cap was whirled aloft on the muzzle of my gun!—while the drivers tore their way into the thicket on foot, and dragged out the second bear to keep company with the first. I was delighted—exalted—overmuch, perhaps!—but my pride was soon to have its rebuke.

"Well," said Splash, slapping his thigh with emphasis, and looking from the bears, which for some moments he had been eyeing, to the piece of ordnance which he had been carrying by way of gun, as if to *that* alone should have belonged the credit of such a shot—"you *are the luckiest man I ever saw in my life!*"

What a damper!—to tell a man who was priding himself on having made a magnificent shot, that it was nothing but luck.

"I'll tell you what, Splash," said I, "to have met the bears was my good luck, I grant you; but to have disposed of them, thus artistically, excuse me!" —and my wounded self-love led me to a recital of incidents perfectly true, yet so nearly akin to vain-

glorious boasting, that *even now* I redden beneath
my visor at the recollection! "It was by good
luck, then, that I once killed two bucks with one
barrel! Loveleap, you saw this! By good luck,
that, at another time, I killed two does with one
barrel!—then, too, you were present. By good
luck that I killed, in two days' hunt, five dear in five
shots—not missing a shot! By good luck that I
killed thirty wild ducks at a fire! (but why speak
of that; any one can shoot in a flock!) It is by
good luck, I suppose, that I throw up a piece of
silver coin, and batter it while in the air, into the
shape of a pewter mug!—or, laying my gun upon a
table before me, fling up two oranges successively
before I touch the gun, then snatch it up, and strike
them both before they reach the earth, one with
each barrel! Luck—luck—nothing but luck! Be it
so; but when you have beaten this shot, and killed
three bears with one barrel, let me know it, I pray
you, and I will try my luck again! But while we
waste time in talk, the scent gets cold. There are two
other bears which took that foot-path there; let us
pursue them—and *good luck* to the expertest sportsman in the field. I shall not fire another shot
today!"

We cheered on the hounds, but they would not
respond. In vain the drivers brought them to the
trail—they would follow the horsemen, but would
not advance a step before them—such was the
instinctive dread they entertained of the bears,

which none of them had seen before that day. Oh, for a bull terrier, or some other dog of bolder nature!—even a cur of low degree, would have yelped in pursuit, and enabled us to add two more bears, perhaps, to the list of slain! But it was useless, and we gave it up when we had tracked them to "Sandy Run," feeling assured that, by this time, they had crossed the Ashepoo, and gained their fastnesses in the hammocks beyond.

We reassembled at the spot, where we had left the bears (henceforward known as "The Bear Stand"); and sending one of the drivers to the plantation for a cart to take them home, betook ourselves to tracking up the wounded buck, in whose favor the bears had unwittingly made so effectual a diversion. The Laird did not seem altogether so confident now, as he had been a few hours before; some slight misgivings as to the success of his shot appeared to be hanging about him, and his companions began to jeer!

"Show us the very spot," said one.

"There," said he; "I was standing behind this log, and as the deer leaped over both at once, I fired!"

"Singed him, no doubt," said one.

"Shot off one leg, at least!" said he, reassuring himself.

"Made capital use of the remainder, however!" bantered a third. "But come—we burn day-light; look for blood, and put the dogs on the trail of the legless buck."

And away went the Laird, hunting for the hoof-print, and turning over the leaves to try and coax a show of blood.

"Here it is!" cried he, as he held up a leaf. "I told you so!"

"Blood?" inquired G——.

"No," said he, "the marrow of his leg!"

"Poh! poh!" said G——; "marrow without blood! —how would you get at it?"

"Marrow!" said he.

"Fudge!" said G——; "but put on the hounds, and they will soon tell who is right."

We brought them to the trail, and it was curious to observe how instantaneously they regained their confidence, when it was no longer a bear to be encountered, but a buck to be pulled down. Away they go for Green Pond—and all the hunters are riding pell mell with the dogs, expecting to see the wounded buck leap from every bush that lay in their way. At Green Pond they turned and pushed into Wright's Bay. How the cry redoubled when they passed over the swampy soil, that had retained the scent more freshly than the high pine land.

"On for Washington's," said Loveleap; "he makes for the river—take up the passes or we lose him!"

And we dash along at full speed, until we occupy the intended stands. We are far ahead of the hounds; but the deer was ahead of us; and when the dogs came roaring by the place where we stood, they swept on in full career for the Chee-ha. There was small chance of their turning, and we ordered our drivers to ride down to the marshes and recover the dogs, if possible, before they reached the river. They were too late. When they reached the bank, some dogs were swimming, some howling on the margin. The deer evidently had crossed, and the drivers sounded their horns in vain to reassemble the pack.

We waited in the road until our patience was exhausted; when, after a weary interval, the drivers reappeared, with but a scanty following of hounds. Dick, in particular, with a subdued tone, reporting the entire Port Royal pack as missing.

"They crossed," he said, "to 'May's Folly,' and having put the river between themselves and him, would not mind his horn!"

"Any blood on the trail?"

"None, sir."

"*Any marrow?*" said another.

The drivers, smothering a laugh, wheel off to the rear without reply; and, to this day, the spot where this remarkable shot was made (and the log is still there to mark it) is called, *the Marrow Stand!*

The high tone of excitement, that had thus far buoyed us up, was now gone. We could not descend from the chorus of the full band, to the piping of the thin straggling cry; nor stoop from bears, and bloodless bucks, to chase, perhaps, a raccoon or a fox!—so we adjourned to dinner!—when, though we eat not, nor drank, like Homer's heroes, we doubtless played our parts without reproach; until at length (to use the strong antique expression), "the rage of hunger being satisfied," we set ourselves to muse, to speculate, and to jest, over the events of the day.

"Apropos of marrow," said C.; "that buck must have been well supplied, or it would have leaked off in so long a run!"

"No more of that, Hal, if thou lovest me," said the Laird.

"His bones are marrowless!" said R.

"And his eyes lack speculation!" I rejoined; "and when I put this and that together, and reflect on these anomalous events, and these seemingly contradictory statements, I confess, gentlemen," said I, with a face composed to seriousness, "that I have strange misgivings about this same buck! His seeming to be shot, yet moving as if unhurt!—his losing a leg, yet running off without it!—his bloodlessness!—*his disappearance at 'May's Folly!'*— the confusion of the hounds—and the unaccountable dispersion of the pack!—impress upon my mind the possibility of this being no deer of flesh and blood— but the 'Spectre Buck,' of which we have heard traditionally, but which I never supposed had been met by daylight!"

"The tradition!—the tradition!" cried several voices, impatiently.

"It is simple enough," I rejoined, "and brief. Some forty or fifty years ago, there lived in this region, then thinly settled, a German, or man of German extraction, named May. He constructed, we are told (just at the place where we so mysteriously lost our dogs today), those embankments, of which the remains are yet visible; and which were intended to reclaim these extensive marshes from waste. They failed of their purpose—involving him in pecuniary difficulty; and hence the name of 'May's Folly,' which the spot yet bears. He became, from this moment, a soured and discontented man; sometimes hunting the deer on these grounds that we have traversed to-day, with desperate energy, as if he would exterminate the very race—and then relapsing into a state of moody listlessness. He grew still more unsocial and secluded as he advanced in life, and men began to whisper strange stories of him. Some hinted that the poisonous influence of French revolutionary atheism had tainted him even in these remote solitudes; that he had mocked at sacred things—respected not the consecrated ground —and even denied the authority and sanctity of the holy book! Others said, that in his moody fits, he had treated his slaves with barbarity; and had shrunk back from the public scorn, which such cowardice is sure to provoke, into the seclusion we have noticed. Be the cause what it may, he withdrew himself more and more from the public observation—until, at last, he died. Then, it is said, that a few of his confidential slaves, to whom he had imparted his desire, complied with his dying injunc-

tions; which were—'to bury his body secretly, in
the midst of these wild and melancholy barrens;
to level the grave, and strew it over with leaves, so
that no man might discover the place of his burial!'
Whether he did this, to mark his scorn of consecrated ground, and of religious services over the
departed; or whether he feared that the slaves
whom he had maltreated, would offer indignities
to his remains; it is useless to inquire. All that
we know is—that he died, and was buried as he had
desired. No headstone marked the spot of his grave;
no prayer was breathed above it—no requiem sung.
At midnight—stealthily, and by the glimmer of a
torch—was he returned to earth; and all was silent,
but the sighing of the night-wind among the tower-
ing pines—as if Nature moaned over the desolation
of her perverse and misguided child!

"The negro looks on this as haunted ground; and
hurries over it, after nightfall, with quickened step
and palpitating heart! Sometimes a gush of air,
warm as from a furnace, passes fitfully across his
face—while a cold shivering seizes on his frame!
What surer token than this, that a *Spirit* is passing
near! Sometimes a milk-white buck is seen, by
glimpses of the moon, taking gigantic leaps—then
shrouded in a mist wreath, and changed, in a twink-
ling, into the likeness of a pale old man, swathed in
his grave clothes—then melting away slowly into
air! At other times, the 'Spectre Buck' starts up
before his eyes, pursued by phantom hounds, which

rush maddening through the glades—yet utter no sound, nor shake the leaves, while they flit by like meteors! It is the ghost of May, doing penance for the sins done in the flesh, under the form of the animal which he most persecuted when living."

"You speak as earnestly as if you gave credit to the legend," said R. "Is it possible that you can believe in ghosts?"

"Doctor Johnson *did*," said I.

"Aye; but he was eminently superstitious, and strained himself into the opinion, because the Scriptures recognized spirits; and he would not be thought to gainsay them."

"Yet," said I, "it is clearly within the competency of God to create ghosts as well as men; beings of vapor, as well as of flesh and blood—sensible to sight, yet impalpable to touch—beings bearing the same relation to man, as the thin vapory comet to the more solid planetary bodies of our system!"

"Yet, to what end," said R., "should they be created? God creates nothing in vain; and what authentic story is on record to show that ghosts, even if they exist, have ever exerted any agency, either for good or evil, on human affairs? Show me that they have served for warning, or for instruction—and I yield the point; but, until then, 'Nec Deus intersit nisi nodus vindice dignus,' is the safer maxim."

"There is great force in what you say," I rejoined; "but how can we reason against the evidence of our

senses. I have not seen ghosts, but I have had
visions!"

The hunters, who were seated loungingly about
the table, playing with their glasses, started at this
avowal, as if a ghost had taken a seat among them.

"Explain!—tell us what you mean!—can you be
in earnest?"

But, before a word could be uttered—

"Ho! ho! ho! ho!" interrupted the Laird, who
had waked up at this moment, from a sort of
"brown study" to which he was subject—and caught
up the thread that we had dropped—"will you
suffer him to gull you at this rate? 'Mark you how
a plain tale shall set him down.' This romantic
story is woven out of mere cob-web. This old May,
whom he would invest with the dignity of a poetical
personage, was nothing more than a sodden-headed
sot, who loved his bottle better than anything in
life; and this is the clue to lead us to the understanding of a conduct not otherwise easy to be
explained. How do I know this? you will say.
Don't bother me, and you shall hear. It happened
that I was galloping after the hounds which were
in pursuit of a deer, in an unfrequented part of
these woods, when, slap! went my horse's legs into
a hole, in which he sunk to his shoulder! while I
took measure of a good slip of land beyond. Having
shaken off the dust, I went to help the horse, who
kept floundering about in the hole; and I then
perceived that he had fallen *into a grave*, which had
caved in under his weight.

" 'A treasure or old May!' said I, and soon began to dig; when I came to—what do you think? At the bottom of the grave, among fragments of a decayed coffin, was stretched out a skeleton complete —and, at its head and feet, by way of head-stone and foot-board, lay—a bottle of *brandy*, and another of *rum*—corked, sealed, and deposited for convenient use, in another world—if, haply, in that world, *drinking* were a permitted enjoyment! And here we have the solution of the incident so ingeniously mystified. The heathenish old reprobate preferred his bottle to his salvation—and looked more to one than to the other, in his last moments!"

"The spell is broken," cried I; "you have disenchanted 'old May' with a vengeance! You have a knack of your own, of getting at *the marrow* of a thing, you know?"

"Confound your marrow!" said the Laird; and bounding from the table, he retired to bed; to dream of hounds that fled, while bears in packs pursued them—of bucks that melted into air, while the death-dealing charge passed through them harmless —of smoke-wreaths, bodying forth the forms of men long dead and moldering—and such like "perilous stuff as dreams are made of."

"And now, that the Laird has gone to rest (if his marrow will let him), tell us of those visions which you spoke of as having been seen by you," said G.; "I have myself been under spiritual influences!"

14—C. S.

"Here it is—all written out," said Venator, with a solemn face, and drawing a paper from his side-pocket; "shall I read?"

"Yes," said G., "especially if it contains your personal experience."

"It is headed *Phantasmagoria*," said Venator—and he read what follows:

"There again! It flits along the wall, a shadowy procession—and now, it seems to pause! Who and what are these bloodless, filmy beings, that move about, yet not like things of life? The human out-line, without the finish! dwarfish, unfashioned—a race of pigmy goblins, sans head and legs! Ho! now they vault and leap! leap legless! to what infernal music, too—all on one sharp key-note. Whiz, whiz—fie ——! I have it! they are little devilets, dancing at a carnival! No! not that either! for they are white, transparent, vapor-like—unlike the imps of darkness! What *are* they? What *do* they? What do they want of *me*, that they thus stop and gibber at me? Avaunt there! Why, that's strange! that's my own voice! I'm not asleep! I'm not dreaming! And yet, *there stand those phantoms* —scared by my voice—huddled into a knot—and writhing in every posture of conceivable distortion! And see! they dance and leap yet higher than before —while their infernal music splits my ear-drum! Now, they waver, as they would fly—then stop— and mock at me! Avaunt, there! *My voice!* yet not *my sight!* Am I awake? Am I an entity, or

something less? a quiddity—or what am I? Am
I myself, or somebody else? Perhaps I'm dead!
Perhaps I'm translated! and, my sins being none
of the heaviest, I am sent to this Goblin Purgatory
by way of expurgation, and the malicious urchins
are dancing me a welcome to their diabolical fra-
ternity! Begone! I'll not consort with ye! Begone,
ye miscreated implets, or I'll sweep away an army
of ye! Begone, thou fragmentary legion! Begone,
I say!"

"Good gracious!" said G., with solemnity, "your
mind must have been deeply exercised. Did they
go?"

"A ray of light," continued Venator, reading,
"enters the chamber, and the phantoms vanish!
But strange! their infernal music is still ringing
in my ears!—fiz, fiz, fie——. A broader ray, and
then an image, gigantic in comparison with the
spectral effigies that had been hovering about me,
enters the room. A lamp is in one hand and a watch
in the other, from which, with spectacles on nose,
he spells the figures on the dial-plate. The image
approaches, touches my hand, which lay nervously
on the bedside, and uttered these cabalistic words—
that dissolved the spell in an instant—and brought
me back from the world of shadows to the world
of reality: 'What are you bellowing for? You'll
wake up the house. It's now two o'clock. You
have swallowed fifteen grains of quinine; your fever
hour is past, and you are a saved man!' 'Whew!

why, Doctor Snorter, is that *you?* I'm glad to see you—very! You're better company than that batch of devils that have been jeering at me all night!' 'They are *my* devils, said he, tapping a phial of quinine which he held in his hand, 'I conjured them up with this bottle!' 'But, doctor, these devils were not black, like those we read of—they were white, very fantastic, and fantastically dressed, too, if I may speak my mind.' 'You might have found them black enough, if you had fallen into their clutches,' said the doctor, rather piqued that the costume of *his* devils had been criticised! 'Then, prithee, doctor, cork them up once more in your bottle, nor suffer them to wander up and down the earth either in black or white! Who knows, when they shall next visit me, whether they shall be white, like these—or like these, be quelled by a word?' "

"Would you have us believe in these visions?" said R., with impatience.

"By no means. Yet I had the testimony of two of my senses to prove their existence; which is more than we have for much that we believe."

"But where does this point? I see neither head nor tail to it."

"How should you? seeing that it has neither."

"What is it, then?"

"*A picture from nature!* I will explain. I was suffering from inflammatory fever—the physician, fearing it was remittent, poured down the quinine— this was adding fuel to the fire. The result was, that the excitement of the brain increased to the point of *hallucination!* I began to see visions, and to converse with unreal personages; yet with a lurking consciousness, all the while, that what I saw *was unreal*, and that the persons presented to my senses *were phantoms!*

"As the paroxysm abated, I awoke to a state of composure, and immediately set myself to write down—before it faded away irrecoverably from my memory—the strange medley, of the real and the unreal, of fact and fiction, of logical deduction and palpable inconsequence, which is here presented you; and which resulted from that condition of the brain to which disease and the doctor had jointly contributed.

"These are the 'insomnia ægri' of which the Latin poet speaks. I have given you a life-like picture."

"Humph!" said the lawyer, with a yawn, "I am sleepy!"

"And now that you provoke me to it, I will say *an original*."

"An 'extravaganza,' I grant."

"Yes, after Fuseli."

But what has become of our missing hounds all the while? *We* have run off, as *they* have done; and must now recover the track of our narrative. The night passed, and nothing was heard of them: the next day, and they did not come; on the second day, a mounted huntsman was sent across the river, to search for them on the opposite side. We have seen, that starting from the Ashepoo, they had crossed the Chee-ha; taking up the search at this point, he traced them from plantation to plantation, until he reached Tar Bluff on the Combahee. At this spot (moistened by the last blood spilt in the revolutionary contest—that of the gallant John Laurens, of South Carolina), he lost all trace of the deer. Whether he swam the Combahee, as he had before swam the Chee-ha; whether he here escaped from the hounds, or was devoured by them; whether he was a deer of flesh and blood, or the phantom buck of the legend—we cannot decide. The data are before our readers; and each one can settle these questions for himself, acccording to his peculiar taste. As for the hounds, they were found (like veterans, as they were) quartered in couples, on the plantations that bordered on their line of march. They were recovered, and returned to their anxious master, who, we fancy, will think twice, before he halloos them off a second time, in chase of a phantom buck, or any buck—whose blood is marrow!

VENATOR.

Come, now, before we part—for we confess to having a kindly feeling for you after keeping company with you so long—come, now, Venator, and tell whether or no you were accounted a successful shot? We are curious to know what you could do with the gun, and how far your companions gave you credit for skill, with the weapon which you seem to have used so freely.

Most readily will Venator answer you—with only this condition—that if he speaks the truth (and in fact he knows not how to lie), you will not accuse him of playing the braggart when he answers your inquiry by a truthful statement of facts.

It seems to him that he has already incidentally answered the question propounded to him; but, if the reader of these sporting anecdotes still desires to know whether the writer of them was esteemed a good shot among his sporting companions—and to have a categorical reply—then the answer must be in the affirmative: for none of them can remember ever having beaten him! He has frequently made even or proportional scores with them—but, since the age of fifteen, he never has been beaten! His *forte* lay in quick firing; and it resulted from this, that in *deer-hunting*, he was eminently successful; when the chance was fair, he seldom had occasion to fire his second barrel.

In shooting birds on the wing—say snipes or partridges—his average scale of shooting was, to bag *eighty-four* to the hundred! He seldom killed more than nine birds without a miss. His best shooting was made when he was sixty-five years of age. This shooting took place at Flat Rock, North Carolina, before witnesses invited to mark his score. Partridges, with a few pheasants and woodcock, were the game hunted—and he succeeded, on *unfavorable ground*, in bagging *thirty-three* birds successively, without a miss! The series was broken by a clear miss at a cock pheasant, which sprung up unexpectedly before him on Glassy Mountain. Mr. William Johnstone, who was in company, will remember it as closing the series. I don't know that he remembers indorsing *that* miss with one of his own!

In early life, the writer of these sports was rather indifferent as to the gun he used. Provided that the lock was reliable, and the barrel straight, it did its work to his satisfaction. At a later period, he indulged himself in a Westly-Richards—14 gauge.

The shooting of which I have here given the record, may be deemed good, or otherwise, according to the skill or opportunities of the reader. The writer is not aware that it has been beaten in this part of the country. But what, after all, is the excellence and precision which the most accomplished gentleman sportsman may attain, compared with the expertness of the sleight-of-hand man, displayed in his daily feats of legerdemain? I remember seeing one of these men plying his trade in the open streets of Paris, in front of the Madeleine, in 1855, the year of the Great Exhibition. He had bought from the authorities, the right to use a little recess of the public court for the exhibition of his sleights. His compensation was the few coppers tossed him by the passers-by, as they stopped to witness his exhibition. He began by spinning a pewter platter on the top of a round stick, and tossing it in the air, then catching it again on the top of his stick; then he spun and tossed a second, and a third, and kept them all three spinning; then passed the stick under one leg, then behind his back; then poised it on his chin, and still kept catching and spinning them at pleasure, without baulk or accident. Then he spun a copper, and tossed it up; then caught that on his round, short staff; and so on with another, until he seemed to exert the same mastery over these small bodies as he had already done over the larger; and concluded, after keeping them playing a long time in the air, by making them descend and lodge in his waistcoat pocket without the assistance of his hands! In witnessing these and other feats of this expert professor of legerdemain, I became ashamed that I had ever prided myself on my accuracy of a shot; since the highest precision which an amateur sportsman can reach, must fall immeasurably short of the exquisite skill acquired by these men in the daily practice of their art. "Non equidem invideo—miror magis."

THE FIRE HUNTER

IT was on a fine evening in October, when the coolness of the air gave promise of an approaching frost, that a man in the common country garb might be observed pacing with hurried step the piazza of his humble dwelling, in lower Carolina. He was short, of sinewy frame, with high shoulders, lank whitish hair, sallow skin, and vulgar features; redeemed from their common-place expression, only by a squint in one eye, and a mouth extending from ear to ear. A crumpled letter was in his hand, and he cast looks of indignation, from time to time, toward a negro boy, who had posted himself without the paling that inclosed the house—as if he feared a nearer approach might expose him to proofs of his displeasure, yet more decisive. The man in home-spun garb was an overseer; the letter was from his employer; and the boy was the plantation messenger, who had just delivered him the letter which provoked his spleen.

"How dared you, sir, tell your master about them bucks that lie in the pea-field?" said the man while a scowl settled on his weather-beaten face.

"Ei, obshaa! you tink I tell?—I know better dan dat; maussa can't tek off de lick, ater you stick um on me! I *got more sense*, I tell you!"

"How, then, could he know anything about them? Who could have told him, if you didn't—tell me that?"

"No me! by gosh! somebody must be see the track where he feed in de pea-patch, and gone tell maussa —if he know about um as you say."

"Clear yourself, you young villain; I'll find it out, if you did tell, and pay you for it, too! Off with you, and send Pompey to me."

The messenger quickly disappeared; and presently the field-minder made his appearance, and touched his cap to the overseer.

"Where are them bucks that live in the pea-field?"

"Enty dey come dere ebery night?" said Pompey.

"Go to the pine barren, get me some of the fattest pine knots, prepare the pan—I mean to go fire hunting to-night."

"But, obshaa!" rejoined Pompey—"maussa count 'pun dem buck for heself. Frost cum, you see, maussa; den cum de question, 'Pompey, whey dem buck? What Pompey guine to say? dey fat for tru."

"Fat or no fat, I have one of them to-night—I'll do it, by jingo, if I have to walk for it. Here he's been writing to me, as if I was a nigger; telling me to keep them bucks till he comes over with his friends to hunt them. Dang me, if I do. Who gave them to him? were they born in his cattle-pen? have they got his mark and brand upon them?

all that have white tails are in my mark, and I'll
shoot them as I please, and ask no odds."

"Dey fatten on maussa peas, anyhow," said Pompey.

"How do you know they're fat?" said the inde-
pendent overseer.

"Case I see dair tracks, and de print deep in de
eart, where dey walk."

"I've seen them, too," said Slouch, "and more
besides than you think for. Who was it, pray, that
took off the rider from the fence, and slipped away
one rail, that they might jump that panel? and
who set the stakes, to snag them, when they were
used to the path? And no thanks to you, that you
did not kill them, for I found the hair on the point
of your stake where it just grazed them in their
leap."

Pompey cast down his eyes, convicted of having
been poaching, on his own hook; and finding further
remonstrance vain, said, with a shrug, "Well, den,
I s'pose I must git the lightwood."

"Certainly; and when the buck is shot, you get a
fore-quarter; but mum! it needn't be known—tho'
I'd do it anyhow!"

In three hours' time, Pompey reappeared at the
house, with tinder-box, lightwood and frying-pan;
while Slouch had caparisoned his raw-boned steed,
and stood ready for service. A sheep-skin, spread
upon his back, was surmounted by a large saddle,
from the croup of which dangled a small rope, with

pulley and tackle attached—so that, sitting on his horse, he might draw up his deer, when once fastened to the cord, without the trouble of dismounting.

Stealthily they took their way toward the field; making a circuit to avoid the watch, whose notice they were not anxious to attract. The night was still and clear; the winds hushed; and the dews lay thick and heavy on the foliage. They passed onward silently, until they approached the spot in which the deer were accustomed to feed.

"The moon is down," said Slouch; "in a half hour they will begin to feed. I'll hitch my horse to this hickory, and we'll raise a fire and go into the field. Let me see!—which way is the wind! D'rat me if it blows at all! That's bad; for if he noses me, he'll snort and be off in a jiffy."

"Eh! eh!" said Pompey, "how he guine to nose you, when you mout and you jacket smell so strong of 'bacca?"

"Damme! if you ain't spelling for a chew!" said Slouch, handing him over a quid. "Now, strike fire, and let's be off."

It was soon done; the blazing chips of lightwood were placed in the frying-pan, and the handle passed over the shoulder of the negro, who swayed it backward and forward, horizontally, with a knowing look, illuminating all objects far and near, except the space kept in shadow by the intervention of the head. It is in this shaded space, that the eyes of the deer become visible to the fire-hunter, appearing like globes of greenish flame.

"Got, Mass Slouch, dat 'ill do!" said Pompey— his love of sport overcoming his hitherto reluctant acquiescence. "S'pose you gee me de gun—I'll slam um ober, I tell you!"

"When did you larn, pray?" said Slouch, eyeing him keenly and not over kindly. "How do you know the distance?—you'd fire before you had got close enough, or scare him by getting too near!"

Pompey looked as if he knew more on the subject than he would readily confess to—while Slouch continued:

"I'll hardly let you scare off this one, I tell you! I know the distance by the size of the eyes; and it took me fifty shots to know that, as I know it now. You'd be for sneaking up till you could see their horns; but an old buck ain't a-going to let you get that close, I tell you. He's the almightiest cunning creature to get round. But, quiet now; for we are getting near. Don't speak a word, but follow me; for I'll keep in the shade made by your body—so throw the shadow right on me."

They now entered the pea-field, nightly visited by the deer; and had advanced but fifty yards, when, at a sudden turn, they came unexpectedly upon a fine antlered buck, feeding upon the tempting vines. He saw—*the men, as well as the fire*—and stamping with his feet, and snuffing the air, which seemed to him fraught with danger, bounded off so suddenly, that Slouch lost the chance to fire. In truth, he was only prepared for a standing shot; and the suddenness of the movement disconcerted him.

"Confound the fellow," said the fire-hunter; "he has cleared himself; but there's two of 'em—and we must keep a better lookout for the second!"

They now moved through the field more warily than before—Slouch in the lead, and Pompey following him close, with a sort of lock-step, so that they cast but one shadow. Presently, by a sign from Slouch, they slackened their pace. He had caught glimpses of a deer's eyes, though yet at a distance; and they continued advancing, but with increased circumspection.

"He's a whacker, I know," said Slouch, "by the distance between his eyes. Don't let's scare him!"

They had now approached within fifty yards, when the deer suddenly lifted his head, and stared directly at the light. Slouch stopped at the instant, drew his gun to his shoulder, and fired. The sound of the gun—the louder, as it seemed, from the stillness of the air—came echoing back from the thick woodland, that inclosed the field like a wall; and the owls, frighted by the reverberation, flapped their wings about the unwelcome light, and hooted to each other in solemn concert.

"He's done for," said Slouch, after a moment's pause. "I don't hear him break."

And the hunters moved to the spot, where a noble buck lay weltering in his blood. They soon turned him over on his back, dragged him by the horns to the fence—which stood at no great distance —and proceeded to clean and divide him. They showed great expertness; and the process did not last long. When they had separated the deer into two divisions, it was bestowed in a long valise-like bag; and, bound with the cord before mentioned, was slung up in a most business-like way behind the saddle of the hunter. And now they were moving from the ground, when a noise attracted the quick ear of Slouch.

"I hear a deer," said he. "He'll stop to look at the light. I'll take the fire, and try if he will stand. You, Pompey, stand by my horse till I fire."

Onward with noiseless step, on tiptoe, Slouch advanced in the direction of the sound: the ground (as they were now outside of the field) was not so open as before—some shrubs occasionally intervening to obstruct the view; but he looked eagerly forward—and catching sight of an eye that glared from the midst of the shrubbery, fired the barrel which he had in reserve. Pompey moved quickly up, to give his help; and came just in time to find Slouch in great confusion, standing over a *fine colt*, that he had shot down by mistake!

"The devil!" said the fire hunter, in dismay; "had it been clear ground, I should never have done that. Pompey, man—see where he's shot."

"Wha use!—he dead as a door-nail," said Pompey.

"What's to be done?" said Slouch, in a tone of despondency. "I shouldn't like to pay for it out of my wages, that's a fact. None but a fool would inform against himself!"

"You far from fool, Mass Slouch?" said Pompey, slily.

"I reckon I am," said Slouch; and flinging off the top rail from the fence, he drove the sharp point of it into the side of the colt, e'er it had well ceased to breathe; and, tickled at the idea of so ingeniously covering his trail, thus continued aloud,— "He'll be a smart chap, now, that'll find out you aint died of a snag!—the pea-field is so inviting— and it's so nat'ral for a young colt to leap the fence after the green fodder! Pompey! keep this close, and I'll make it up to you! You needn't know anything about it, nor miss the colt, till day after to-morrow; and, by then, I reckon, my shot-holes will tell no tales!" And he chuckled, as he thought, how the harpies (his allies) would, long before that time, whet their beaks in the carcase of his victim, and obliterate by their loathsome orgies, all traces by which his participation in the death might be detected:

"Contactuque omnia fœdant-
Immundo."

In a few minutes, the worthies are on their way home; and Pompey was preparing for an expedition, better suited to the darkness that encompassed them, than to the too searching glance of the midday sun. They approached the settlement unperceived; for the watch, as in duty bound, was, by this time, fast asleep!—and the haunches and loin of the buck were carefully bestowed in a sack, while the fore-quarters were reserved for the fire hunter and his associate.

"Now, Pompey! start off with this venison, and carry it to the stage-house, and give it to Snug the driver; and tell him to take it to town, and leave it, he knows where. Tell him to keep back his part of the money, and send me the things I spoke for, out of the balance."

"Leetle 'bacca for me, Mass Slouch?"

"Certainly, Pompey."

"An' mus' I tek your hoss?"

"No! day-light may catch you on the road; and I don't wish my horse seen there. Take the old mare; that will keep her from whickering after her colt. And, do you hear, Pompey—when you're coming back, just turn into Softhead's field and let the creetur go inside. If they knock her brains out, I don't care; and she'll be out of sight for one day, any how! So off, Pompey, and make no stay."

We shall now leave the faithful Slouch, after having acquitted himself thus honorably of his trusts, to retire to his rest; which, we may assure the reader, was disturbed by no qualms of conscience—while we follow Pompey on his mission to the stage-house.

Everything went according to his wish—the mare was lashed into a brisk gallop; Snug received the venison; and Pompey, rewarded by a dram and a slice of cavendish, set out on his return. When he had now got near his home, he turned off the mare within the fence of Softhead, as he had been directed; and took a cut-off path through the woods, to save himself the trouble of a longer walk by the road. And now, when he had well-nigh completed his journey, he was brought to a pause by observing the remains of a fire near the path, of which the embers were yet burning.

"What's dis?" says Pompey; "here's been somebody fire hunting tonight, besides me. Ah! ha! here 'tis! dey tro out de lightwood down here! wonder what dey kill!" and he kindled the fire with the splintered pine, which blazed like gunpowder. "Here's de frying-pan, by jing!" said Pompey, as the rising flame illuminated everything around; "dey must hab kill something, or dey wouldn't throw away de pan!—hog mabe!—mabe calf—for calf eye, when meat scarce, shine so like deer, ee tek a bery honest man to know de difference! Ecod, I look out; mabe I ketch someting wot while!"—and flinging the blazing fagots into the pan, he proceeded on his way, examining the road for some signs, by which to guide him to what he sought. "Ho! ho! I on the right course now;

for dere de horse track—and here de blood!—ee
point for home! Mass Slouch may be, double
behind my back, and gone out gen; one buck! one
colt! he want more meat—dese buckra man greedy
for tru! Well, I on the trail now, and I find um
'fore long!"

The negro's attention was soon arrested by the
distinct sounds of a horse's tread, which seemed to
proceed from the path directly ahead, and which,
indicating at first but a slow pace—came suddenly
to mark the movement of a horse at speed.

"He run from de light," said Pompey; "you at
some debiltry, is you?" and he hastened forward to
reconnoitre the spot, from which the horseman had
so hurriedly sped.

The spectacle that met his eye was anything but
what he expected! Lying across the path, and
turned over upon his face, was the body of a man,
whose suppressed groans, and writhing limbs, gave
token of the agony that tortured him. Pompey set
down the light, and turning over the fallen man,
had no sooner looked into his ghastly face, than he
screamed out, "My God! my brother!—oh, who
has done dis ting? Tell me, Toney; as God is me
judge, I'll kill um! Dat dam Slouch done it, aint
he?"

Toney shook his head.

"Who den?"

The wounded man made signs to Pompey, to
raise him up to a sitting posture. His shirt and

jacket were soaked in blood, and his hand was pressed upon his breast, which had been pierced by shot. The lung had been wounded, for the blood flowed from his mouth as he essayed to speak, and threatened immediate suffocation.

"Tell me," said Pompey, as he supported his head on his shoulder, and bathed his face with his tears, that fell like rain; "how dis cum?—who done this?—who kill my brudder?"

Toney pointed to the neighboring plantation. "He done it, but not on purpose!"—and with many interruptions, the dying man communicated to his brother, the particulars of his misfortune, which were briefly these: His wife was sick, and he wanted to buy some sugar for her, but the distance to the store was great, and he thought it would be no harm to take the mule from the stable, and ride there to make his purchase. Having placed his sack of corn on the mule, and exchanged it for the sugar, he was, on his return home, attracted by a light in a field which lay on the route, and supposing no danger, and led by curiosity alone, he rode up to the fence, and was looking toward the light, when he received the shot in his breast, which struck him to the ground. On recovering, he found ——— standing over him, and lamenting himself for having killed him. He begged his forgiveness: and told him he had mistaken the eyes of the mule for those of a deer! Toney had begged to be taken home to die, but the fire hunter, selfish to the last, and fearing that his agency in the matter would thus be exposed, had refused to do so, until he had exacted a solemn pledge from him that he would not divulge who had done it. The pledge given, he placed him on the back of the mule, and was thus leading him home, when, startled by the approach of the torch, he suffered the wounded man to fall from the mule, and mounting himself, rode off to escape detection.

The story of the poor fellow's misfortune was rather gathered from hints and broken sentences, uttered in the intervals of pain, than from any connected narrative, which, from his failing strength, he was incapable of giving.

"Bless God, me brudder, dat you find me here! Tis berry hard to die alone, in these dark woods! Life is sweet, me brudder. Oh! dat God would let me stay here longer! But, I see how 'tis!—I must go—I feel it at my heart! Maussa musn't say I die like a tief!—tell um all 'bout it! If he bin here, de fire hunter neber bin shoot me! Feel in me pocket, brudder—take out de paper wid de sugar. Oh! me blood upon it! Neber mind!—gib it to me poor wife: tell um to 'member me!—tell um, for him sake I get me death! I'm cold—draw me to the fire."

And the poor fellow stretched himself out—his head sunk upon his brother's breast—and he was a corpse.

NOTE.—The practice of fire hunting, forbidden by the laws, is nevertheless but too much pursued in certain parts of the country. It is the author's aim, in this narrative, to expose the dangers to property and to life, attendant on this illicit practice. It is nearer akin to poaching than to legitimate hunting; and he professes no personal acquaintance with it. The sketch here given, unlike those that precede it, must be considered as illustrative of life—rather than as "a sketch from life." The melancholy incident with which the narrative concludes, is nevertheless true; and came within the range of his personal observation.

OF THE ANIMALS OF CHASE IN SOUTH CAROLINA

The title of our little book suggests the propriety of saying something of those animals which are the objects of chase with our sportsmen. These are the black bear, the deer, the wild cat and the fox. To these might have been added, some years back, the panther, the wolf, now nearly extinct; and, upward of a century ago, the buffalo; which, as Catesby informs us, was, about the year 1712, found in herds within thirty miles of Charleston.

The maritime portions of Carolina and Georgia were well calculated, when in a state of nature, to give shelter and protection to these denizens of the forest; being intersected by frequent streams, and covered, especially among the swamps, by a dense undergrowth of shrubs and creeping plants, that made pursuit impracticable. But, in the progress of events, these things are much changed; the impervious swamps have been subdued to the culture of rice; the high lands have exchanged their forest honors for maize and the cotton plant; and these wild animals have been destroyed, or driven from their fastnesses, to seek more sequestered haunts. Accordingly, no living man has seen a wild buffalo in our confines. It is a rare thing to encounter a panther (the skin of one, killed by the late Col. Blanding, is preserved in Charleston). The wolf is almost extinct; the bears are fast diminishing in number; the deer, though still numerous in given sections, are visibly thinned; and it is only the smaller animals, such as the foxes and wild-cats, which are still numerous, or whose diminished numbers have not been made the subject of remark.

THE BEARS—Are not often made the objects of a hunt. They frequent the deep swamps, into which, in ordinary seasons, the sportsman would scarcely be willing to penetrate. If pursued in their fastnesses by dogs, they would either beat them off, or escape by clambering trees. There is little chance of killing them, except when caught on their marauding expeditions. To these they are often tempted by their fondness for the ripening corn, on which they commit nocturnal depredations; and in default of this, their favorite food, being omnivorous, they sometimes attack the droves of hogs, as they feed, in the wooded swamps. The young ones fall easy victims; but the older sometimes escape, after suffering terrible lacerations from the claws of their formidable foe. The stag or fox hound, is not readily induced to pursue the bear. On two occasions, only, have I seen them put to the proof; on one, they actually *skulked*, bristling up their hair, and showing insuperable repugnance to proceed. On the other they did manage to screw their courage to the sticking place; but soon left the

chase, with alacrity, to pursue a deer that crossed
their trail. In such a chase, the cur is superior to
the hound. The largest bear I have seen in the low
country, was shot by my friend, Colonel Ashe, of St.
Paul's. He has had him well preserved; and the
visitor is startled, on entering his country mansion,
to find his effigy, erect and life-like, keeping sentry,
as it were, in the hall. From these particulars, the
reader will infer, that the bear, though sometimes
encountered by accident, is too seldom to be found,
and too hard to be approached, to be made an
ordinary and regular object of sport!

THE WILD-CAT—Abounds in the lower country of
Carolina. He frequents the deep swamps, covered
by almost impenetrable thickets. He seeks his prey
chiefly, but not exclusively, by night. He is very
destructive to partridges and wild-turkeys, to rab-
bits, and sometimes fawns. When these fail him,
he invades the poultry-yard, the pig-stye, and the
sheep-fold. Lambs of six months old are killed,
and carried off. Such is their strength, that they
have been known to kill one nearly full grown, drag
it over a fence four or five feet in height, and remove
it to a neighboring thicket. A planter residing
within five miles of Beaufort, found, on visiting
his sheep-fold one morning, that a sheep was missing, and on examination, discovered the trail by
which it had been dragged off. Setting on his
hounds, they soon discovered the sheep, half

devoured, in the thicket—and near by, the felon, in
shape of a wild-cat, so gorged with his meal that
he could make no run, and was quickly dispatched
by the dogs. If they do not frequently destroy the
full-grown sheep, it proceeds from caution, rather
than from want of strength to do so. Here is an
incident in point. A tame doe, two years old, had
been so severely bitten by dogs, that it died of its
hurts. As I was riding one evening along a ridge
of wooded land, I perceived it where it lay dead—
and, on the following morning, directed my servant
to bring it home, as food for my hounds. He surprised me on his return, by telling me that the deer
was not to be found where I had directed him to
search for it. Whereupon, I rode myself to the
spot, and found that the deer had been dragged off;
and following the trail, which was plainly to be
traced, by the leaves and earth, I discovered it
covered by leaves, and half consumed, on the margin of a pond full fifty yards distant from the place
where it had lain. Neither was there any doubt as
to the manner in which the removal of the deer
had been effected, for the footprints of the cat were
plainly and deeply impressed in the soil, along the
entire line of the trail—the only doubt which could
arise, was whether the removal had been effected
by one, or by more?

In hunting the wild-cat, we do not scruple to use
the gun: first, because he sometimes climbs the
trees, and thus defies the dogs—and, secondly,

because, if brought to bay and suffered to fight it out with the pack, he seldom fails to cripple the boldest and finest hounds. His fangs are long and sharp, and his jaws have strength enough to crush the bones of a dog's leg.

The wild-cat, when pursued by hounds, endeavors, like the fox, to baffle them by frequent doubling; but unlike the fox, he keeps to the thickets, and makes his run among the most tangled and impervious covers: so that it is difficult for the sportsman to get a glimpse of him. Where it could not be rode into, I have adopted the plan of leaving my horse on the edge, and making my way on foot, into the heart of the thicket. If, pursuing the same plan, you should remark the hounds running upon one of the fallen logs (in which these grounds usually abound), the probability is that the cat, in his next double, will take precisely the same run. By placing yourself so as to command a view of the log, the chances are that you will shoot him. I have often adopted this expedient with success.

A full-grown wild-cat will sometimes succeed in beating off a half dozen dogs; though I once owned a noble hound who would kill a cat single-handed. I was witness to such an exciting contest. I was hunting cats, with my two well trained cat-hounds, Rowser and Black, and had given the cat a chase of a couple of hours, when Black, having been thrown out, Rowser brought the chase to bay in a hedge. Seeing but one dog in pursuit, he determined to give battle, and after a growl of defiance, left the cover of the hedge, and leaped out into an open field. Rowser sprang after him, and the cat, instead of flying, threw himself upon his back, raised his head, and extended his fore-paws in the attitude of a pugilist *on guard*. The dog approached, (his hair bristling upon his back), and stood almost over his recumbent foe. There was a pause of several seconds, during which they glared upon each other with inconceivable fury, before they closed in the death struggle. The dog seized the cat on the breast, between the fore-legs; the cat, at the same time, burying his fangs in the shoulder of the dog. Though bitten through and through, he uttered no cry of pain, but pressed down upon the cat—nor relaxed his hold until his foe was dead. He killed him *by dint of pressure;* for his tooth had never entered the skin of the cat—(nor have I ever witnessed an instance in which, when killed by dogs, their skins have been torn by their teeth.) The instinct which taught the dog to destroy his enemy, *by pressure*, must be deemed not a little remarkable. When the cat was dead, his fangs still remained clinched in the shoulder of the dog: his jaws had to be separated by force, and the victor, released from his grip, was unable to move, and was taken home on the back of a horse. I need hardly add, that I never suffered this gallant hound a second time to engage single-handed, in so serious a conflict.

If, in the combat just described, the cat did not aim at the throat or other vital part of his adversary, we must ascribe it to accident—not to any defective organization; for I believe this animal to be endowed with the instinct of destructiveness, in the highest possible degree. On what grounds, I shall presently explain.

When yet a boy, I witnessed an incident in point, which made an impression on me that can never be effaced. An uncle, resident in Beaufort, received from his overseer in the country, a present of a young wild-cat. It was very young indeed—was evidently but a few days old—and scarcely exceeded in size the common domestic kitten. It was treated with care, and when able to run about the yard, a small box was fitted up for its reception; from which it sallied forth at pleasure to take the liberty of the grounds. It was now observed, while yet a tiny thing, creeping after the poultry, and endeavoring to spring upon them. To check this disposition, a cord was fastened round his neck, and a clog attached to the end, so that when he made his spring the weight would draw him back, and prevent his doing mischief.

My uncle one day invited several of his friends, to witness this development of natural propensity in his savage pet. The kitten, with his clog attached, was let out of the box; and it was curious to observe with what stealthy pace he approached the spot where the poultry were feeding. They scarcely seemed to notice the diminutive thing that was creeping toward them; when, crouching low, and measuring exactly the distance which separated them, he sprang upon the back of the old rooster and hung on by claw and teeth to the feathers, while the frightened bird dragged him, clog and all, over the yard. After several revolutions had been made, the cat let go his hold on the back of the fowl, and, with the quickness of lightning, *caught the head* in his mouth, clinched his teeth, shut his eyes, stiffened his legs, and hung on with the most desperate resolution, while the fowl, rolling over in agony, buffeted him with his wings. All in vain! In a few seconds more he was dead, and we looked with abhorrence on the savage animal, that had just taken his first degree in blood. In this case, there could have been no teaching—no imitation. It was the undoubted instinct of a cruel nature! We wondered that this young beast of prey, should have known, from this instinct, *the vital part of its victim!*—and we wondered still more, that in the providence of God, he had seen fit to create an animal with an instinct so murderous. Philosophy is ready with her explanation, and our abhorrence may be misplaced, since from its very organization, he is compelled to destroy life *in order to live!* Yet, knowing this, our abhorrence still continues; whence we may draw the consolatory conclusion— that the instincts of a man naturally differ from those of a wild-cat.

THE FOX.—The red-fox is not found in Carolina; the grey abounds; and, if the country be favorable, may be taken by a good pack, in a run of a few hours. Fox-hunting, as pursued in England, is but little practised in the section of country with which I am most familiar—viz., the belt bordering on the sea-coast. The country is too much intersected by swamps, and covered by a growth of tangled underwood, to admit of rapid riding; most of it, indeed, is impracticable for a horse. But in the middle country, where the ground, comparatively open, is more favorable to equestrian exercise, the sport is followed with great spirit by the Hamptons, Taylors, Singletons, Mannings, and other familiar names. Intimately connected with an indulgence in this manly sport, comes the rearing of a superior race of horses, and the practice of feats of dashing horsemanship. It is from this section of country, in the event of war or civil commotion, that our cavalry will be supplied with officers as efficient and accomplished as ever graced the service of a state.

OF THE BIRDS WHICH ARE THE OBJECTS OF SPORT

Of the birds which are the objects of pursuit with the sportsmen of Carolina, the principal are— the wild-turkey, the partridge (perdrix marylandica), the dove, the golden plover, the woodcock and snipe. Of the aquatic birds, we shall name two varieties of wild geese—a great variety of ducks, including some of exquisite flavor—and numerous sea-plovers and curlews, which, though sometimes shot, are, from the nature of their food, seldom admitted to the table.

THE WILD-TURKEY—Is found in considerable numbers; but everything connected with the modes of shooting them, or capturing them, has been so often noticed by others, that to refer to these topics here, would seem to be but a useless repetition. They breed in the country, and are not very sensibly diminished in numbers.

THE PARTRIDGE—Is the same bird which is miscalled in the Middle States, the quail. It is a veritable partridge—though smaller than the English partridge, or the red-legged partridge of Spain. Eaten in October or November, when just full fledged, and fresh from the gleanings of the pea-

field, they are a great dainty, though I am not
prepared to bestow on them the same extravagant
commendation as was given by an enthusiast to
the red-legged bird of Spain—viz.: "that it should
be eaten with none but champagne sauce, and in no
posture but on one's knees—through thankfulness."
This bird, delicate as it undoubtedly is, is not
more valued by the epicure, on the table, than by
the sportsman in the field. The coveys leave the
thick covers during the afternoon, and feed in the
open land, preferring the pea-fields to all other
range. They stand the point in these open grounds,
until the hunter approaches as near as he pleases,
and yield him capital sport. They breed in May,
making their nests on the ground, and laying as
many as twenty-one eggs. If my observation serves
me faithfully, I should say, that unlike all or nearly
all other game, they have increased instead of
diminishing with the clearing of the country. The
extensive grain fields furnish them with ample
subsistence; and it may be, that while man has
increased *his* means of annoyance, *that* from birds
and beasts of prey has, in greater proportion,
decreased. They are particularly numerous along
the sea-coast, and among the *cultivated islands*. The
saw palmetto plant, which abounds among these
islands, furnishes them an admirable protection
against hawks, which are their most destructive
enemy. I once received, from a Spanish merchant,
a present of a pair of red-legged partridges. I

built for them a latticed house, apart from the homestead, and hoped to have propagated the race among us; but some beast of prey broke through the lattice by night, and destroyed them. I see no reason why they should not be propagated in this region and latitude. The experiment could advantageously be made, by some gentleman who is sole proprietor of an island; for he would have ample means of security against poachers, and might thus prevent the premature destruction of the coveys. Let me hope that my hint will not be lost, and that some gentleman will succeed in naturalizing them.

THE DOVE—Is strikingly like the wild pigeon in plumage and form. It differs from it in being smaller, and again, in being far superior in richness of flavor and tenderness of fibre. Though it breeds in the country, it is far more numerous in winter than in summer. The pointer notices them; but they will not stand the point, so that the most approved method of shooting them is for several gunners to take the field at once and fire as the birds cross to their feeding or resting-places. I think there is no falling off in the numbers of this bird. They feed on the grain left in the fields by the reapers, and on the seeds of grasses (crab grass) growing in the cotton-fields.

THE WILD PIGEON—Makes us but occasional visits, only I suppose when it has devoured the mast and

other food, which in ordinary seasons it finds in
more northern latitudes.

THE PLOVER.—This is none of the aquatic variety.
It visits Carolina in April, for a few weeks, on its
way north. It is then thin, and of little culinary
value. It returns in August, in such capital condition, that being shot at an elevation of twenty feet,
it bursts open from the fall. It is remarkable, that
in one and the same day, you will find them spread
along the line of the Atlantic sea-board—over a
distance of one thousand miles! We will take the
20th of August for example; and we shall find,
that from Newport, Rhode Island, to Savannah,
Georgia, plover shall be seen! They frequent the
high, open pastures; and I have never found them
on any grounds but such as were browsed by cattle
—whence, I conclude, that in some way, they provide them with their food. They are a shy bird,
and are best approached from a carriage.

THE WOODCOCK AND SNIPE—Are birds of passage.
The first are rarely found in numbers, except where
the hard frosts of the north have driven them hither
for subsistence. The snipes are more numerous,
arriving in October and remaining until May.
Their numbers appear to me to have decreased
greatly of late. I cannot ascribe this altogether to
the improved condition of our agriculture, as especially shown in the superior drainage of our swamps;

since morass enough remains to furnish subsistence to millions; nor can the havoc made among them, by sportsmen, account for it. It occurs to me that they must be disturbed at their breeding-places, or destroyed in the egg.

OF WILD-GEESE—The smaller variety is much esteemed, while the larger is in little request; its flesh being hard, and often fishy.

OF WILD-DUCKS—We have, in winter, a great abundance; though these, in the opinion of observant sportsmen, have likewise sensibly decreased. One, only, is native—the summer duck, or duck of the woods; the others retire on the approach of summer. The duck and mallard, the black-duck, the blue and green-winged teal, the raft duck, the switch-tailed widgeon, and the summer duck, are greatly esteemed for their flavor. This depends on the quality and abundance of their food, which consists, besides various living water grasses, of the acorn of the quercus virens; the kernel of the lotus; the seeds of several species of reeds and aquatic plants; above all, *of the rice*, which has shelled in the field during harvest. There is a constant tendency in this grain to degenerate into the *volunteer rice*—a variety, in which the pearly white color, so valued in commerce, is changed into the red; and which has the further peculiarity of shedding the grains before the fields are ripe enough for the

16—C. S.

sickle. Thus, an unfailing supply of the choicest food is provided for these winter visitors, who show great adroitness in billing up the fallen grains from the fields, when overflowed. When shot, their craws are found loaded with rice. It may be heresy to dispute the supremacy of the canvas-back duck of the Susquehannah, but I must say, that such as venture as far south as 32° and 33°, are not equal in flavor to the rice-fed duck of this region. It may be said, that the canvas-back is "off of his feed"— and it may be true!—but I doubt his superiority, taken at his best. What the old English divine said of the strawberry—"doubtless God might have created a better berry, if he had chosen—but, doubtless, God never did"—may be applied "nomine mutato," and, I trust, without irreverence, to the rice-fatted wild-duck of Carolina; "doubtless God never did create a better duck!" Besides those already enumerated, we have varieties of widgeon, some equivocal, some fishy; not to speak of the salt water kinds, with serrated bills, which, formed to feed upon fish, obey their calling—and, for culinary purposes, are neither fish, flesh, nor fowl. These, with curlews, sea-plover, and the like, are shot, but seldom eaten—since all the condiments of a Spanish cuisine would fail in overcoming the disagreeable flavor that gross feeding has communicated to them!

RANDOM THOUGHTS ON HUNTING

THEY take, it seems to me, a false as well as a narrow view of human life, who denounce all amusement and recreation, as unworthy of accountable and immortal beings. The transition from exercise to relaxation seems to be a requirement of our mental as well as our physical constitution: and (to adopt an illustration, which, however trite, is exceedingly pertinent to our matter), as the bow which is never unstrung, however excellent the material of which it is composed, soon loses its elasticity, and comes to be utterly worthless—so fares it with the individual, who, forgetful of this law of his nature, would keep either mind or body in a state of constant tension! The history of man, in every phase of his existence—in every stage of his progress, from the grossest barbarism to the highest pitch of refinement—shows that *amusement*, under some shape or other, is indispensable to him. And if this be so, it is a point of wisdom, and it is even promotive of virtue, to provide him such as are innocent. Field sports are both innocent and manly.

In these remarks I am far from pretending to the discovery of new truths; I am simply desirous to recall public attention to such, as, sufficiently well known, are at times strangely overlooked—especially by our ascetic innnovators, who would make

life as unjoyous as their own natures; who would
reform society, by denouncing dancing as a sin—the
theatre as an abomination—and all amusements,
however innocent, as a waste of time unworthy of
immortal beings! These are the men of a single
idea, who, placed in a valley, bring everything to
the standard of their own limited horizon—who
refuse to look beyond, unless superciliously, through
the medium of a prejudice so inveterate, as to dis-
color or distort whatever is graceful or beautiful in
nature or art. And their error, it seems to me,
springs from this intense self-esteem—and their
utter inability to get beyond themselves, so as to
understand the relations and wants of others. They
look at life from one position only—and refer everything to their own standard. Students—philosophers, it may be—having their time at their own
disposal, to labor or relax, just as it suits their
humor, they cannot realize the fact, that *their*
relaxation would be none to the grosser and less
refined masses of society; and that amusements that
employ the senses, are needful to restore *their* worn
bodies, and revive their wasted spirits—that they
are happier and better for the relaxation that follows the day of labor. It is with the same persons,
and from the same mistaken views, that we find the
severities of the Jewish sabbath ingrafted, without
warrant from the Scriptures, on the Christian
polity.

Instead of proceeding on these false assumptions: 1st, that society can dispense with amusements; 2d, that all amusements are a sin, how much wiser, how much worthier of those whose lives are exemplary, that they should encourage by their countenance such amusements as are innocent and elegant—*dancing*, for example—and by this countenance, preserve it as it should be, the handmaid of modesty and grace.

Instead of purchasing up theatres, to convert them into churches (which only causes new theatres to be built), it would be wiser, it seems to me (since every civilized Christian community has indulged, and will doubtless continue to indulge, in theatrical representations), *to reform these exhibitions*, until they should present nothing to the public, but what the most scrupulous delicacy would approve! How far this may be done, will be evident to those who will be at the trouble of examining the plays of the elder dramatists—of Ford and Webster, for example —and comparing them with such as are now exhibited. Few of these but would be hissed from the modern theatres, if represented as originally played. Nay, even those of Shakspeare and Jonson, if played from the original copies, would share the same fate, along with many masterly efforts of Beaumont and Fletcher, and Otway and Dryden, which their indecency has banished from the stage. And, indeed, to such an extent has this reform proceeded, that you may chance to hear fewer things offensive to delicacy, in our theatres now-a-days, than in some pulpits that could be named—wherein vice is stripped with so determined a hand, that decency revolts at the exhibition—(as if modesty were unscriptural, and the maxim, "pudorem illum superandum esse," were now, as formerly, the rule of the church)—and those passages of Scripture, which men scruple to read aloud in the presence of their families, you may hear so paraded and dallied with before the congregation of the young and pure in heart, that the indignant blush of shame is seen mantling their innocent cheeks! Comprehensive as the *Decalogue* assuredly is, there is yet nothing in it akin to indecency; and it seems quite possible to exhort man to the performance of his duty toward God and toward his neighbor—and to chastise his vices, too—without lapsing into indelicacy! Yet, since such things do happen, who but a madman would apply himself to pull down the pulpits thus desecrated, instead of purifying them of their gross offences? This is true wisdom; this is the true rule! Let it be applied to the theatres; and while their immoralities are frowned upon and repressed, let not the world lose the instruction and delight which they are calculated to impart!

As to country amusements, it seems to me, that they who denounce them should withhold their censures, until they can substitute a recreation more commendable than hunting. So far as physical education is concerned, it stands preëminent. Its manliness none will deny; neither is there wanting

ground for supposing (startling as the proposition
may seem) that its tendency is actually promotive
of good morals. For, whether it has happened by
accident, or whether it stands in some unexplained
relation of cause and effect, I know not; *but the
fact is so*, that of all the associates who have acted
with me in field sports, and were interested enough
to excel in them, not one has been touched with the
vice of gaming! Men of fortune, men of leisure,
peculiarly exposed, from their social position, to
this most demoralizing vice, have been completely
exempt from it. May this not be ascribed, in a good
measure, to their devotion to this pursuit; and to the
indirect influence of some of those habits of thought
and action that it calls into exercise? Here is *the
forecast*, that provides, at a distance, for what may
be wanted at a given day—the *punctuality*, that
observes the hour and day appointed—the *observation*, that familiarizes itself with the nature and
habits of the quarry—the *sagacity*, that anticipates
its projects of escape—and the *promptitude* that
defeats them!—the rapid glance, the steady aim,
the quick perception, the ready execution; these
are among the faculties and qualities continually
called into pleasing exercise; and the man who
habitually applies himself to this sport will become
more *considerate*, as well as more prompt, more full
of resource, more resolute, than if he never had
engaged in it! Assuredly, there is no such prepa-
ratory school for war; and the expert hunter will,

I doubt not, show himself the superior in the field to another, every other way his equal, yet wanting this experience! Neither should I forget to mention, among its recommendations, the direct tendency of this amusement to promote social intercourse, and the interchange of friendly offices between neighbors.

Thus thinking of the value of amusement in general, and of hunting in particular, I cannot but perceive with regret, that there are causes in operation which have destroyed, and are yet destroying, the game to that extent, that, in another generation, this manly pastime will no longer be within our reach. Sportsman as I am, I am not one of those who regret the destruction of the forests, *when the subsistence of man is the purpose.* It is in the order of events, that the hunter should give place to the husbandman; and I do not complain of it. It is the wanton, the uncalled-for destruction of forests and of game, that I reprehend.

Undoubtedly, the most obvious cause of the disappearance of the deer and other game, is the destruction of the forests, that of the river swamps, especially; which being, in their original state, impracticable to horsemen, secured them against pursuit; for, if pressed by the hounds, they could escape by swimming the rivers. These lands being cleared and cultivated, no longer afford them refuge. The same applies, though with less force, to the thickly wooded high lands cleared for the culture of cotton. Their feeding and hiding-places being more contracted, they can more easily be hemmed in and destroyed. The uncleared lands, too, bordering on the cultivated portions of the country, are much less densely covered with undergrowth than formerly. The contrast is so striking, the change undergone within the last twenty years so very apparent, that I have been induced to inquire into the causes which have produced it. It is mainly to be ascribed to the rearing of increased numbers of cattle, for agricultural purposes; to the trampling and cropping of the shrubs and undergrowth by these extensive herds; but, above all, by the practice of burning the woods in spring, to give these cattle more luxuriant pasturage. By these causes combined, so great a change has been wrought on the surface of the land, that the sportsman may now dash along at half speed over a country, which, but a few years back, he could not traverse on horseback. While in this way, his power of intercepting the deer in their flight has been greatly enlarged, it will not be denied that, in the modern improvements in gunnery, his means of annoyance have been immeasurably increased.

The demand which has grown up in our cities, for the supply of hotels and of the private tables of luxurious citizens, with venison, has called into being, a race of professional hunters, who, settling themselves wherever the game is abundant, and cultivating merely corn enough to maintain themselves, their horses and a couple of hounds, devote their days and nights to hunting. Their profits are greater than accrue from the cultivation of the soil; and the freedom from restraint enjoyed in this kind of life, is more congenial to their tempers. It is too much to expect of this class of men to refrain from "fire hunting," though forbidden by law. Who can detect the offender? or who would become informer, if the trespass was not committed by entering his own inclosure? In a few years, the game is destroyed, or driven off. *Our* hunter follows them to their new retreats, pitches his tent, or builds his cabin in another quarter; and re-commences his career of destruction.

The incessant hunting of their grounds by proprietors, may lead to the same result; but the sport, in their hands, is not apt to be pursued so recklessly, or carried to the extent of extermination—except when the overseer takes it up for the six months during which the proprietor is absent. In this case, the landholder soon finds that his grounds provide him neither with amusement nor supplies.

The right to hunt wild animals is held by the great body of the people, whether landholders or otherwise, as one of their franchises, which they will indulge in at discretion; and to all limitations on which, they submit with the worst possible grace! The "feræ naturæ" are, in their code, the property of him who can take them—irrespective of any conflicting right in the owner of the soil. In the sections of country well stocked with game—where, consequently, the temptation to hold such opinions is the strongest—the feeling on this head is so decided, that some overseers refuse to accept a place (otherwise desirable) if they are restricted in the right to hunt. The writer of these pages, finding that during his absence from his property, his game had been destroyed, and his interests, in other respects, sacrificed to this propensity of his overseer—insisted, at some cost to his popularity, on inserting a clause to his annual contract, absolutely restricting him in this respect. And what was the result?—that having made his own grounds, by this restriction, *a preserve*, they were only the more harassed, on this account, by the unrestricted in the neighborhood—who took a malicious pleasure in destroying the game which a proprietor had presumed to keep for himself.

Though it is the broad common law maxim, "that everything upon a man's land is his own—usque ad cœlum"—and he can thus shut it out from his neighbor without wrong to him—yet custom, with us, fortified by certain decisions of our courts, has gone far to qualify and set limitations to the maxim.

The land which he has purchased with the proceeds of his industry—and for which he pays tax to the State—is no longer his (except in a qualified sense) unless he incloses it. In other respects, it is his neighbors', or anybody's. It is true, that he may proceed against another who cuts his timber, though it lies beyond his inclosure, as a trespasser

—yet the same man may turn a drove of cattle on
these lands, and browse on, and trample them, to
the destruction of a hundred times the value—without risk to himself, or leaving any chance of redress
to the proprietor and tax-payer. In like manner
may a man's land be "harried,"—and not only his
game, but sheep and other stock, be worried by the
dogs of hunters, traversing his uninclosed grounds
at discretion, without his being able to protect himself, as matters now stand, or obtaining any legal
redress for the injury. It seems a questionable
policy—in a country peculiarly situated as ours is—
thus, by construction of law, to diminish the value
of land, and the inducement to hold it, by limiting
and narrowing the rights of proprietors. Yet the
poor man, who owns no land, is slow to perceive
the beauty or fitness of the common law maxim;
and the demagogue is not the man to point it out.
He has but one purpose—*to gain the favor of the
people!*—his means, not the elevation of their
nature, by instilling high and generous feelings,
but the flattery of their prejudices—a flattery as
obsequious and as abject, I grieve to say, as that
which, in monarchical governments, is lavished by
courtiers on a monarch, or on his minion! They
have but one policy—they steer but one course—
and that is, *with the stream.* If you catch them
departing from this course, it is because their tact
has been at fault, and they have unwittingly mistaken an eddy for the main current. The right

to hunt uninclosed lands, thus secured by usage, or in other words, by *our* common law—there are some who desire to extend it to inclosed lands, unconditionally—or, at least, maintain their right to pursue the game thereon, when started without the inclosure. It is to be apprehended, that this spirit of encroachment is but too much fostered by such of our public men as, setting popularity above everything, fear to hazard it by publishing truths unpleasing to the majority! We admit, without hesitation, that there are in Congress, *patriots* who see the *right* in the *expedient*—and the *expedient* in the wishes of their constituents. Nor is there any sufficient reason for thinking that Congress enjoys a monopoly of this sort of virtue. Restrictions on this unchecked right of hunting, in communities circumstanced like ours, will, therefore, I presume, be slow in coming by the legislative enactment of laws conservative of game; and if the laws were stringent, the juries would be indulgent and slow of giving damages, except in cases of flagrant injury.

During the session of the court, held in the southeastern circuit of this State, I was present at a trial which will serve to illustrate the state of public opinion in reference to this subject. It was an action for trespass, growing out of the conflicting rights of the hunter and the landholder. One of the hunters was on the stand. He was himself a landholder, and a man of some property, and the question was put by the counsel:

"Would you pursue a deer if he entered your neighbor's inclosure?"

Witness—"Certainly."

Counsel—"What if his fields were planted, and his cotton growing, or his grain ripe?"

Witness—"It would make no difference; I should follow my dogs, go where they might!"

Judge—"And pull down your neighbor's fence, and trample on his fields?"

Witness—"I should do it—though I might regret to injure him!"

Judge—"You would commit a trespass; you would be mulcted in damages. There is no law for such an act!"

Witness—"It is hunter's law, however!"

And hunter's law, is likely somewhat longer to be the governing law of the case in this section of country; for the prejudices of the people are strong against any exclusive property in game, as every one feels who attempts to keep it to himself. Several gentlemen of my acquaintance have been proprietors of islands; which were a source of perpetual annoyance to them. No sooner were they stocked with game, than the *amateurs*, if not the *professed poachers*, would find their way to them; and if a bailiff was employed to keep them off, he often proved, as in other countries, the principal poacher. And, if actions of trespass were brought against intruders, the results were generally unsatisfactory. Juries are exceedingly benevolent in such cases; and even should conviction ensue, the fine or imprisonment of a freeman for so trifling and venial an offence, as shooting a wild animal, would be deemed a measure of odious severity!

Nor does the proprietor fare better in his attempts to fence out depredators, if his possessions are situated on the main land. Admitting that he *can* impose a light fine on the trespasser, found hunting within his inclosure, the proof is very difficult, and the penalty insufficient to deter from a repetition of the offence. Besides, the poacher may injure you scarcely the less, while he keeps himself free of the legal toil. He whistles a dog into your preserve, at night, or at early dawn, and lurks in the neighborhood, until the deer, startled from their fancied security, leap the inclosure and become his prey. Or, should your fence be so strong and high as to prevent the escape of the deer, a torch thrown into the dry brush-wood, during the high winds of March, envelops it in flames, and your labor and expense are made unavailing by a casualty (so called) which, nevertheless, you feel to have been a design—though you cannot legally prove it! In this instance alone, the principle of the anti-rent excitement is at work with us!

With this single exception, the rights of property are as religiously respected in our community, as in any other that can be cited; and I am of opinion that the unwholesome condition of public sentiment in this particular instance, is mostly an affair of inoculation. It is derived from the laboring emigrants from England, who, mixing with the operative classes of our own white population, inspire them with their own deep disgust at the tyranny of the English game laws. When they descant upon the oppressions which have driven them from home, to better their fortunes in this land, this seems to be the sorest and best remembered of their griefs—transportation, for killing a hare or a partridge! The preservation of game is thus associated, in the popular mind, with ideas of aristocracy—peculiar privileges to the rich, and oppression toward the poor! What wonder, then, that men, forgetful of the future, surrendering themselves to the present, mingle with the throng of destructives who seem bent on the extermination of the game; rather than attempt the difficult, and unpopular, and thankless office of conservators!

I think there will be a reform in this matter—not that I shall witness it. It must be the work of time. When the game shall have been so killed off, that the mass of the people shall have no interest in hunting their neighbors' grounds—the law will be reformed; and when that same time arrives, the juries will have no interest in construing away the law. So that we may yet hope to see the time when men may, under the sanction of the law, and without offence, or imputation of aristocracy, preserve the game from extermination—and perpetuate, in so doing, the healthful, generous, and noble diversion of hunting.

THE END.